Other Books by Dr. Timothy S. Stuart

Children At Promise

(with Cheryl G. Bostrom)

Raising Children At Promise

**HOW THE SURPRISING GIFTS OF
ADVERSITY AND RELATIONSHIP
BUILD CHARACTER IN KIDS**

Dr. Timothy S. Stuart
Mona M. Stuart

JOSSEY-BASS
A Wiley Imprint
www.josseybass.com

Published by Jossey-Bass
A Wiley Imprint
989 Market Street, San Francisco, CA 94103-1741   www.josseybass.com

Jossey-Bass books and products are available through most bookstores. To contact Jossey-Bass directly call our Customer Care Department within the U.S. at 800-956-7739, outside the U.S. at 317-572-3986, or fax 317-572-4002.

Jossey-Bass also publishes its books in a variety of electronic formats. Some content that appears in print may not be available in electronic books.

Library of Congress Cataloging-in-Publication Data

Stuart, Timothy S.
    Raising children at promise: how the surprising gifts of adversity and relationship build character in kids / Timothy S. Stuart and Mona M. Stuart.
      p. cm.
    Includes bibliographical references.
    ISBN 978-0-7879-7563-0
    1. Child rearing—Religious aspects—Christianity.
2. Parenting—Religious aspects—Christianity. I. Stuart, Mona.
II. Stuart, Timothy S. Children at promise. III. Title: Children at promise.
IV. Title.
BV4529.S88   2005
259'.2—dc22

                               2004019600

FIRST EDITION
PB Printing   10 9 8 7 6 5 4 3 2 1

Contents

To our dear children and best teachers,
Tyler, Ian, and Moriah

Acknowledgments

Special thanks to the Rehoboth Community, whose compassion and love for children humbles and blesses us, and to the teachers and students of Rehoboth Christian School; Julianna Gustafson and the entire Jossey-Bass team for your friendship, editorial wisdom, and belief in the At-Promise message; Mark Kerr for suggesting this workbook; Linda Wagner for your gentle strength, prayerful guidance, and professional expertise; Rob and Laurie Teasdale and Peter and Jodi Reek (our Breakfast Club), Lynda Burke, Janet Weeda, and Ron and Colleen Polinder for caring about these pages as only friends can; our parents, Jim and Sharon Janz and Walt and Patricia Stuart, whose love astounds us more each year; and to our dear friend Cheryl Bostrom, who has kept company with us all along and who encouraged us to write together. Along with the anointing of our Heavenly Father, these friends have seen us through, and we bless you all.

Raising
Children
At Promise

Introduction

The ultimate goal of *Raising Children At Promise* is to settle you into a deeper hope for the kids you love. It aims to bring you to a point of faith and confidence about the promise your children possess regardless of the circumstances they face. Perhaps strangely, that confidence will result from taking an honest, personal, and intimate look at your fears, concerns, and difficulties with children, not just at your highest hopes for them. We encourage you to transfer the energy you may now spend over-protecting, rescuing, worrying about, and maybe even avoiding kids into building trusting and expectant relationships with them, knowing that all children are made to be Children At Promise.

For too long we've pretended that difficulty and frustration must be banished from childhood (and parenting) so that kids can grow well, avoid risk, and sidestep the possibility of failure. For too long we've emphasized programs, budgets, organized activities, and structured achievement over relationships. But if we're honest, we'll admit that the greatest shaping in our lives has come out of our own painful circumstances and our positive relationships. The At-Promise perspective offers us a way to view kids so that both their trials and their trusting relationships with caring adults can strengthen and fulfill their promise.

In *Raising Children At Promise* we invite you to take an honest and transforming look at your parenting, teaching, or mentoring journeys with kids. More than that, we ask you to wrestle with your assumptions about how kids grow best and how adults best support and encourage that growth. We hope you can feel our personal pulse in the questions, stories, reflections, and answers that lie ahead. For like you, we hunger to set things straight in our lives, to go deeper, and to become wiser companions and better interpreters of adversity to children. Writing this workbook has given us the privilege of pursuing that course. Through it, we've taken the book

Children At Promise out for a very long spin—top down, kids crammed in the back seat, radio blaring, open road ahead. The workbook is filled with discoveries from our yearlong test drive and blazes a trail for your own At-Promise adventure, which can begin right now, if it hasn't already.

The truth is, in our eleven years of marriage, ten years of parenting, and fifteen years as educators, nothing has shifted our worldview as a couple, transformed our assumptions about children, or focused our parenting as much as the At-Promise paradigm. However, our shift to At-Promise thinking also inspired—even provoked— in us a surge of important new questions, something all new paradigms should do. For instance, How on earth do we live this out with our own three kids every day? With students? What implications does it have for schools, frustrated parents, and youth programs? Have we committed to growing PROMISE character in ourselves? How do we do that? How do we make sure that we don't merely "love" the At-Promise concept but live it—truly and authentically? Our need to chase down these answers for ourselves compelled us to write this workbook and convinced us that others would benefit from such a quest as well.

How to Get the Most out of This Workbook

This workbook is meant to be a companion to *Children At Promise: 9 Principles to Help Kids Thrive in an At-Risk World* by Timothy S. Stuart and Cheryl G. Bostrom (Jossey-Bass, 2003). Each workbook chapter corresponds to a parallel chapter in *Children At Promise,* so you'll want to pick up a copy of the book if you haven't already. Reading it will not only ground you in the theory and rationale behind the workbook, but we think it will also inspire you to apply its perspective to your relationships with kids.

From the start of this project, we set out to create a workbook that people could finish and would want to finish. Here are the elements we included to help you stay the course for your greatest personal benefit:

- *A Balanced Workload.* We intentionally crafted each chapter to include some sections that demand thought, reflection, observation, and journaling ("Connecting" and "Barriers and Breakthroughs") and others that inform, feed, and encourage you ("Real Life: Where the Journey Begins," "Striking the Flint," and "Cutting to the Chase").

- *Character Assessments and At-Promise Profile.* We also designed an At-Promise Profile at the back of the workbook where you can record the scores of up to four children on nine separate character assessments. These assessments give you an initial snapshot of how strong or weak the various AT PROMISE attributes are in your children and assess traits like perseverance, optimism, integrity, and service. By completing each one, you'll obtain an overall profile of each child that helps you see where you can grow stronger together through relationship.

- *Observation Guide and Journal.* Although observation and journaling can strengthen our understanding of children, many of us never get around to recording our insights about kids. To give you a jumpstart in that direction, *Raising Children At Promise* includes weekly Observation Guides. Each guide focuses your attention on one aspect of the At-Promise perspective and encourages you to notice how you and your kids, grandkids, or students relate to each other, face difficulty, and are growing in PROMISE character. As you step back to observe your children each week, you'll record your observations in a separate notebook or journal. Buy any type that makes you want to spend time writing in it. Find one worthy of holding your most honest and personal observations about the kids in your life. And make sure you carry it with you where you can observe your kids best—on the sidelines of the soccer field, in your classroom, at the park, in the car, or in your very own living room. By clipping a favorite pen to the outside cover, you'll always be prepared to jot down a spontaneous thought or revelation.

The Breakfast Club: A Group Approach

Making room for At-Promise thinking in your life is going to change you. It's going to shake up your view of the world. It's going to radically alter how you see and mentor children. We encourage you to create or seek a natural and supportive group of fellow adventurers to travel through these changes with you. Maybe you already belong to such a group and can introduce *Children At Promise* and this workbook into the mix. Just make sure you gather people you want to learn from and grow with and who are eager to grow themselves.

During the three-year gestation and writing of *Children At Promise*, we met every month or so with a group of friends we dubbed "The Breakfast Club." The group started as an attempt to maintain the camaraderie of three childhood friends

(Laurie, Jodi, and Mona) and their subsequent husbands (Rob, Peter, and Tim). Warm cinnamon rolls, Starbucks coffee, and fresh fruit salad guaranteed buy-in from the guys. We rotated houses and included all our kids.

This group of friends helped us, and continues to help us, wrestle through the nitty-gritty of At-Promise thinking. Around the breakfast table on Saturday morning, in each other's yards, sitting on sofas, we navigated the depths of *Children At Promise*. We asked questions, tested the theory by throwing out examples from real life, made connections between At-Promise principles and our own childhoods. We debated and affirmed the concept and considered the promise and struggle we saw in each other's kids.

Your group might consider debriefing on each chapter of the workbook after you have completed it, introducing the "Conversation Starters" from *Children At Promise* (pp. 165–168), sharing your Observation Journals or creating your own unique format that works best for your group. Think about inviting fellow educators or youth workers, parents from a playgroup, other adults who share your situation (single parents, grandparents, working moms, stay-at-home moms, home-school parents), friends in your neighborhood or from church or work, or even a couples group you initiate (with a realistic meeting schedule). If none of these options fits your life, or you feel you need to work through these issues privately as a parent, couple, or caring adult, consider yourself a member of our Breakfast Club. There's certainly room in it for you.

ONE

The At-Promise Perpective

Some parents welcome their children into the world with ease. Others experience the struggle of parental love even while tasting its early joys. Still other courageous souls must stare hard through a tunnel of surgeries, unsolved diagnoses, deformations, illness, personal depression, or other complications to capture even a tiny glimpse of a promising future for their children. Most parents, though, know a good mixture of both pleasure and pain while raising their children through life's varied and unpredictable seasons.

And each of us, knowingly or not, uses a personal paradigm to interpret the meaning of the events our kids face—a framework that helps us understand life's goodness and its devastations. Make no mistake. These paradigms have the power to quietly shape how we and our children live. Whether your journey with kids so far has been easier than you thought it would be or more difficult than you ever imagined, the At-Promise paradigm can help you live with hope for your kids and with trust in God's pledge of love and promise for every child.

In Chapters One, Two, and Three, we'll take a new look At Promise, consider our own At-Promise stories, and examine the fears that prevent us from freely committing ourselves to children and to growth. As you begin, remember that promise is a powerful word. When applied to a child, it says that God makes an unconditional vow, an oath, a pledge, a commitment to love and uphold that child through things to come and to heal a child from things past. It is a word of assurance and confidence that holds us steady while all the plans and purposes God has secretly imbedded in a child come to life through love, trust, and trials.

"God is not a man, that He should lie, nor a son of man, that He should change His mind. Does He speak and then not act? Does He promise and not fulfill?" (Numbers 23:19).

CHAPTER 1

A New Look At Promise

You don't throw a whole life away just 'cause he's banged up a little.

—Charles Howard Smith in *Seabiscuit*

People, even more than things, have to be restored, renewed, revived, reclaimed, and redeemed; never throw out anyone.

—Audrey Hepburn

On a wintry Saturday morning in New Mexico, my seven-year-old son, Ian, handed me (Mona) a piece of red construction paper with nineteen soldiers drawn on it. He asked me to cut out eighteen of them for the paper castle he and his twin sister were making. The nineteenth had an X drawn across it. I trusted his assessment, disregarded the X'ed-out soldier, and started cutting out the rest.

The twins joined me, and soon clippings littered our hardwood floor. Before long Ian made an unfortunate stray cut, shaving off a chunk of one soldier's head. Just as I might have, he muttered, "Well, that one's ruined." But his sister Moriah rushed in, grabbed the soldier out of his hands, and convincingly said, "No, Ian, you didn't mess him up. He's OK!"

She worked deftly, re-forming the soldier's head with her plastic scissors. "Are you saving that soldier from the trash, Moriah?" I asked. "Yeah. Ian thought he messed him up too bad, but he's not ruined. He'll still work. See?" With a confident smile, she held up a soldier that looked amazingly whole.

We continued cutting out the rest of the army as the kids chattered about the little red men. Moriah said, "If his arm is torn off a bit, just pretend that his arm was cut off in a battle, OK, Ian?"

"But what will he do if he has to climb walls? He'll learn to climb walls with his other good arm?" "Yep."

I finished cutting my stack of soldiers. Moriah moved on to the nineteenth soldier Ian had drawn, the one I had cast aside. "And even though someone put an X on this guy," she said, "he can still be saved. Look. He's fine. He doesn't have to be thrown out."

Maybe you can relate to how I began that Saturday morning. Cutting paper with my kids because they asked me to, lulled into thinking that paper soldiers have little significance. But after only fifteen minutes of play, Moriah's perspective on those soldiers and on her brother awakened me and dignified those paper cutouts—especially the one with the X.

Most of us, in our effort to carve out a life for our families, have cut some corners by failing to discipline our kids or by indulging them. At times we've wounded or hurt our children, snipping important pieces that leave them a little disfigured—or a lot. Certain parents have been diligently exact, doing everything in their power to train their children "just so," until suddenly, an intruder—a schoolyard bully, a shady friend, or perhaps alcohol, pregnancy, or pornography—grabs hold of their work and defaces it, instantly cutting parent and child to the quick. Still others are secretly tempted to draw an X through a child who pains them (maybe in pencil, not in ink just yet) because the despair and futility run so deep. There have been times, for us at least, when we pencil the X on ourselves, feeling our inadequacy so keenly, convinced we're bungling our own children.

The at-risk movement loves these X's and specializes in convincing us that our kids are headed for trouble when adversity of any kind hits home. But imagine the relief you'd feel if a trustworthy person were to walk into your family's scattered clippings and say, "Wait. These kids aren't wrecked. They can make it. You thought they were messed up for good, but they're not ruined. Things can still work. Let me show you how you can see kids differently—with hope. Even though someone penciled an X on this guy, he doesn't have to be thrown out. Look! He's going to be just fine."

This visionary outlook sees more in kids and in ourselves than meets the eye. It believes in and looks for promise in every child, no matter how tattered or flawed that child may appear. It acknowledges pain's agony but also its gifts—of growth, of character, and of hope. It notices and invests in children. It replaces busyness and avoidance with real connections with kids. It offers hope to defeated and fearful families. It's called an At-Promise perspective.

Changing Our Minds

Here's the problem. Most of us learned to approach kids like I approached my Saturday morning with my children and their soldiers. We've been lulled into thinking that the way we categorize people or the X's we place on them have little significance. As uncomfortable as we might be with writing off kids or using the at-risk vocabulary, we're not aware of any alternatives. If a three-year-old's mother dies of cancer, landing him in a trail of foster homes, isn't he at risk? What else would he be?

Even those trying to curb the overuse of the at-risk label among educators, policymakers, or parents can collapse into fatalism. Listen to this profoundly wistful, if not hopeless, conclusion that one writer offers on the subject: "In some cases, of course, [we] genuinely may not know what a person's real risk is. That is a sad fact—not about . . . jargon, but about life. Often, people really are simply headed into trouble, and we can't say exactly what that trouble might be. Would that it were different. But when it's not, perhaps at-risk truly is the best we can do."[1] The helplessness and hopelessness of that last line burns in us as we write this book and as we work with kids. It keeps a fire for change alive in us because leaving kids at risk is certainly not the best we can do. Don't get us wrong. We don't deny the risk. We don't deny the wounds. But with a God who makes all things possible, kids must be more than the sum of their risks.

Still, we live in a risk-laden society and have quietly developed an at-risk mindset without knowing it. So what has this at-risk education taught us? We've learned that pain is bad and that avoiding it at all costs presents our best chance for raising healthy kids. We've accepted that some kids are "destined for failure" and others are "headed for success," based on what they have and don't have. We've been led to believe that while relationships and faith are important, material provisions, enrichment programs, Baby Mozart, and "a good, solid education" really provide the best antidotes for most problems. And we've swallowed all this like a drug recommended for all by the FDA. Everyone's taking it, so we might as well take it too.

But frankly, it's impossible to raise children At Promise without rejecting at-risk thinking. We have assumptions to wrestle with—assumptions about risk and children that need to be pinned to the mat. When the wrestling match is over, nothing short of hope will come from knowing that God intends promise to overcome risk in all who bear His image, children grow through challenges when supported by people who aren't afraid of them, and the "No's" in children's lives—no to walking without a limp, no to growing up without a father, no to living without the gawking stares of curious people—aren't as powerful as the "Yes!" that God speaks over them through His promises (2 Corinthians 1:18–22). The larger "Yes" spoken by a child's Creator is this: "Yes, you matter to me. Yes, I made you. Yes, your life has purpose and promise in my eyes. I say 'Yes!' to you."

The At-Promise Concept in a Nutshell

The rest of this chapter gives you the speed-dial version of the At-Promise paradigm (in case you haven't read *Children At Promise* or just want a refresher before plunging into the deep end).

The At-Promise paradigm is summarized in the following acronym:

A—Adversity and trials that lead to growth

T—Trust between a caring adult and a child

P—Perseverance

R—Responsibility for actions

O—Optimism

M—Motivation from identity

I—Integrity

S—Service to others

E—Engaged play

Two influences shape every child's (and every individual's) life: adversity (pain) and relationships (people). Kids will only engage life and contribute positively to their world when they experience *both* the power of love and the pain of trials; one without the other will limit character growth and success. Adversity without trusting relationships can cripple kids. Trusting relationships without adversity can indulge them. But when the two intersect, watch out! That's when the greatest of all growth happens in our children and in us.

That's why the AT combination stands alone in the AT-PROMISE acronym. It's only when adversity and trust meet in a child's life that their promise can be fulfilled. Take note if you've assumed that cramming only beauty and safety and opportunity into your child's life will lead your child to success. Without some form of adversity in his or her life, a child's success becomes extremely fragile, and so does the child.

Of course, not all adults deserve a child's trust, no matter how charming and devoted they may appear. That's why we expect adults to get serious about their own growth if they want to help children grow too. Effective mentoring requires self-reflection and change. And so the second section of the acronym outlines the seven attributes that each adult should seek to possess and to pass on to children, the PROMISE characteristics of perseverance, responsibility for actions, optimism, motivation from identity, integrity, service, and engaged play. Thankfully, as we submit to love and to growing through trials, these characteristics forge themselves deep within us. They're not an end in themselves but rather the outgrowth of adversity and relationship.

Each of these seven PROMISE attributes also correlates with a child's success. Does that mean that if a child has integrity and serves others, he'll become a prestigious CEO or a Rhodes scholar? Not necessarily. But without question, he will contribute positively to the moral and social fabric of society. After all, that's the At-Promise definition of success: positive contribution, not acquisition (of wealth, education, or status). It's exhilarating to look for, pray about, observe, and cultivate PROMISE character traits in our kids. By doing so, we set our children up to shine in this world—to contribute instead of being defeated by circumstances or being wrapped up in acquisition for its own sake.

Road Map for the At-Promise Journey

If you're thinking, "This At-Promise thing has to be a process," you're right. Character and relationships are slow-growth investments. Adversity weaves itself in and out of life unpredictably. We can't combine all three elements at will and expect overnight results. No. The At-Promise journey could easily last a lifetime if we're going to love kids from beginning to end. It requires changes that take time—like overcoming our fears of pain and commitment, which are worthy of leaving behind but take work to abandon.

The kicker, though, is that promise emerges on God's timetable, not our own. And there are no guarantees that we will see every child's promise in full bloom on this side of Heaven. Hebrews 11 reminds us how God prizes the faith of people in this situation throughout history: who are certain of what they hope for and confident of what they don't yet see. These people of faith were commended for fixing their eyes on a country they had not yet visited—the Promised Land—and believing in its reality though they hadn't experienced its fulfillment. They suffered great hardship, but "all these people were still living by faith when they died. They did not receive the things promised; they only saw them and welcomed them from a distance." The writer to the Hebrews concludes, "The world was not worthy of them" (Hebrews 11:13, 38).

Perhaps in your lifetime ten children—or twenty, or two—will burst into your sight with such convincing promise that you will fix your eyes on who they truly are no matter how contradictory their behavior or circumstances might be to that vision. Our calling is to act on the promise we see. Not to work miracles, not to rush change, not to deny the troubles that come along, but to love and to believe against the odds. Though we may never see the promise in some kids (not even with "magic eyes"), we must know and believe that it's there just the same (in high definition and Technicolor, no doubt). We must honor God's workmanship in their lives and encourage others to look for what eludes us, because promise waits to be recognized in every child.

CHAPTER 2

Telling Your At-Promise Story

Although it's easy to concentrate on our children's growth and our children's promise, this journey is about the caring adults as much as it is about the kids. Only when we reconcile At-Promise thinking with our own experience can we apply it with confidence to our children. So this chapter is about you. It gives you a chance to identify, reflect on, and articulate how people and pain have uniquely shaped your life and, beyond that, to see how they've contributed to the fulfillment of your own promise.

A Case in Point

Chapter One of *Children At Promise* begins with the late Larry Burkett reflecting on his childhood (p. 9). Until I (Tim) interviewed him, Larry had never pieced together his own At-Promise story. In fact, because he assumed that At-Promise children had prizewinning childhoods, he wasn't sure he qualified to be interviewed for the book at all. And so he began our talk by saying, "I don't know why you want to interview me. I don't have any fuzzy stories to tell you about my youth. I barely had a childhood."

As it turned out, Larry Burkett not only had an At-Promise story to tell, but his story captures better than most how pain and people can work together in a child's life to create a future of undeniable contribution. The pain—Larry had stored it away, and he wasn't in the habit of talking about it. The relationship—with a high school teacher named Dan Blackwell—came back to him almost like a picture in a forgotten yearbook, though it signaled a major turning point in his life at one time. These pieces of his past had faded for him, but his resulting climb into the role of a cherished financial and spiritual counselor made a permanent impression on millions.

Good Grounds for Storytelling

You may be thinking, That's the way it should be. Let's look at results. Why sift through our past hurts and relationships (even positive ones) when we're perking along just fine right now?

That's certainly a legitimate question. Why look back? Why bother unearthing our past to tell our own At-Promise story? Here's why.

1. Our story can give hope to kids (and parents with kids) who are living through the struggles we faced. Who in your life might be encouraged to know what you've overcome? What are the hidden lessons in your failures, your hard knocks, your heartaches? What's been forged in you? What still hurts way too much or still needs healing? There are more Larrys in the world than we can imagine. They and their families need to know that God has a future for kids who struggle.

2. Our story can honor and acknowledge the contributions of others to our lives. Just think of the hope that Larry's story gives to teachers and youth workers because of Dan Blackwell's investment. A few hours of math tutoring a week and an interest in an overlooked kid. After Dan's contribution, Larry never looked back. The way our stories model gratitude is valuable to kids and adults alike. Who do you have to thank for a positive turning point in your life? Who saw more in you than you saw in yourself? Who pointed you to a future so big that you had to grow into it? Who welcomed you into their family, their community, their circle? Who gave you a place to call home? Have you ever mentioned these people to your kids, students, grand-kids, friends?

3. Our story can help us put our kids' stories in perspective. We can get so caught up in a given chapter of a child's life that we forget God is writing a story of epic pro-portions in that child—a story that isn't close to being finished. We've all wandered. We've all learned by hitting walls. As painful as it is to watch, our kids will too. Our stories will remind us that God is after our hearts, not our neatly packaged lives. We may need to ask ourselves, What did it take for me to yield to God's healing and love in my life? *Have I even done that yet?* What did I willfully run after before facing my need

for change? How many detours have I followed, and yet isn't God still finding ways to spray-paint His love for me on billboards, to call me into the path of *life?*

Redeeming Regret

You see, our stories are about contributing hope, compassion, and courage to *others,* not just about excavating our *own* pain or personal relationships. Many of us are driven by black marks in our past. Places to which we don't want to return. Experiences that will "never happen to us again"—or to our children, for that matter. Though we insist that these horrible events, experiences, or relationships are behind us, much of what we do is motivated by their lingering sting. We simply cannot open ourselves up to the possibility of that pain ever again. But what if these events didn't detract from but added to our making? What if the good in us can partly be attributed to our darker moments? And what if these moments could be redeemed so their sting was removed for our healing and our peace? Telling our story can set this process in motion. Yes, recognizing our story may mean returning to some "if only's" in our lives. If only that didn't happen. If only my life hadn't been compromised by that choice, that person, that experience—a marriage, an abuse, an accident, a failure, a decision, a grief, a sibling, a parent, an illness, a disability, a loss, a hurt, a betrayal, a child. But our prayer is that your return will lead to the healing of your regret.

Sometimes we wish we could just start over so we could "get it right this time, from the beginning." But we are clay. We are useful only because of what goes into our making—the good, the bad, and the devastating, too. This wouldn't be true if we were in the hands of an amateur potter, but we're not. "O Lord, you are our Father. We are the clay, you are the potter; we are *all* the work of your hand" (Isaiah 64:8; emphasis ours). Let's allow that consolation to work on our hearts, and let's look at our own At-Promise stories—trusting that God will rewrite them from His perspective as we do.

Making Sense of Your Story

With these motivations in mind, answer the following questions. They will tease apart the trusting relationships and the trials you've experienced, as well as the growth that resulted from them. Don't rush yourself through this. You may need to reflect on some questions while going about your daily business and then return to the workbook to fill in the blanks. The goal is to hit on the truth no matter how long it takes.

Children At Promise explains, "Each person's life is marked in one way or another by relationship and adversity. Some grow up in relatively supportive, caring, and healthy environments; others recall childhoods devoid of support and blistered by difficult, adverse, or even abusive experiences. Many fall somewhere in the middle, knowing a good dose of both love and pain in varying degrees over a lifetime" (p. 12).

1. Was your childhood characterized more by loving relationships or adversity (or a mixture of both)? Where would your childhood fit on the continuum shown here?

   Relationship———————————————————————————Adversity

2. Which people captured your attention in your youth (up to age twenty-five or so)? Which ones woke you up to new possibilities in yourself or your future? These could include extended relatives, teachers, coaches, bosses, church or activity leaders, family members, or friends. Think of the great people who inspired you in your youth. Who were they?

3. What "hard knocks" got your attention in your youth (up to age twenty-five or so)? What experiences woke you up to the painful realities of life? Your "hard knocks" might include things like your parents splitting up, getting cut from the basketball team, losing your job or your girlfriend or boyfriend, failing a grade, suffering a consequence, getting pregnant, or being injured, sick, overlooked, abused, or kicked out of school. Think through the "eye-opening" experiences of your youth. What were they?

4. Did any of the positive relationships or difficult events you described in questions 2 and 3 spark a turning point in your life? Which ones? What happened?

"If your childhood was more characterized by nurturing relationship, then we suspect that times of significant growth occurred when you encountered and dealt with difficulty. If your childhood was more characterized by pain and adversity, then we suspect that your turning point resulted from someone stepping into your life at a particularly difficult time, believing in you, and offering you hope" (pp. 12–13).

5. Which was it for you? What pushed you into the greatest character growth you've experienced so far? (Keep in mind that the catalyst for growth—whether relationship or adversity—may have occurred well after your childhood.)

A Moment for Your Memoir

Using your previous answers as inspiration, choose one time in your life when either a positive relationship or some kind of adversity propelled you into growth and change. What happened? How did it happen? What were the results? How did a relationship and adversity intersect in that experience? Outline your story in the space below, or write it out in your Observation Journal. Then share it with your Breakfast Club members, your spouse, or a trusted friend. *This story will probably be just one of many in your life, but telling it will give you an opportunity to see how relationship and adversity work together to shape us for good again and again.*

A Prayer for Perspective

Father—Potter—you look on the events of my life with compassion and hope. You don't even look for clay without lumps and defects, because you know it doesn't exist. You take me as I am and work your miracles in the good, the bad, and the devastating. Thank you for being an expert and not an amateur. I simply cannot trust the raw stuff of my life to just anybody or begin to believe it's a part of your workmanship unless you are *perfect*, absolutely trustworthy, unfailing, powerful, forgiving, good. I surrender my story to you. All of it, beginning to end. And I ask you, Lord, to use it to encourage, strengthen, and give hope not only to my own soul but also to children and other people who need it. I trust you to continue using the people and the painful experiences in my life to bring out my true self, which is already exquisite and award-winning in your eyes. I know that the promise in every child is already mapped out in your mind. It has been since the beginning of the world. Lord, let me be a part of calling it forth and displaying it to the world for your Glory. Amen.

CHAPTER 3

The Trailhead

Fear Versus Love

Every time I take a step in the direction of generosity, I know I am moving from fear to love.

—Henri J. M. Nouwen

Getting Ready

We begin here, at the crossroads of fear and love, because our journey depends on which one of these will triumph in our relationship with kids. Fear cripples relationships and keeps us from contributing. Love releases us to give and focus on others. In this chapter we'll uncover our fears together, get a good look at how they affect our lives and the kids we love, and have a chance to surrender them. Before we start, though, if it's been more than a week since you read Chapter Three of *Children At Promise* ("Fear: Love's Counterfeit"), review it now.

Connecting

After reading the Fear chapter, jot down your personal response to it. What grabbed you, made sense to you, or connected with your experience? Was there a breakthrough—some new discovery—about how fear has affected your life, home, children, family?

Approach Avoidance

Perhaps you're familiar with a floating, restless anxiety in your gut—a general concern that your child could take a wrong turn or get into big trouble. Or maybe your anxiety is more specific. You fear that your daughter will sleep around, your son will never recover from your divorce, or your children will struggle horribly because of illness, anger, relocation, or some other factor.

No matter how vague or specific your fears might be, the question is, do you really need to expose them? Will admitting them do you any good? Or will voicing your fears (even to yourself) simply morph them into self-fulfilling prophecies? Isn't it safer to leave the phantoms in the closet where they can't come true?

King David, one of the most admired and candid rulers in history, struggled with these questions. He agonized over whether to hide or expose his troubles and fears. The Psalms reveal an interesting pattern, though. When David hid his troubles from God, he withered; when he exposed his anxieties to God, he flourished. Ultimately, David chose disclosure over secrecy as his modus operandi for life. When he was stalked, tormented, and threatened, he refused to allow fear's adrenaline to drive him for long. Instead he voiced his fears, pursuing God's attention with a raw honesty that eludes most of us in prayer. David reassures us of the outcome. He says, "I sought the Lord, and he answered me; he *delivered me* from *all* my fears" (Psalm 34:4; emphasis ours). Not just a few of his fears. Not just his entry-level worries. No. *All* of them.

So how honest should you be about your fears in this chapter? Well, you should be as honest as you want to be free. God's love meets us when we tell the truth.

> The Lord is my light and my salvation—
> Whom shall I fear?
> The Lord is the stronghold of my life—
> Of whom shall I be afraid?

—Psalm 27:1

Real Life: Where the Journey Begins

On a Monday afternoon, our son Ian ran home, bursting through the door to tell us that his twin sister, Moriah, was in trouble. Tim raced to find her across the school campus where we live. Ten minutes later he returned, his voice vacant and serious as he called me into the kitchen. I (Mona) rounded the corner and saw Tim's arm around a whimpering, shivering girl, soaked in mud and pond water, standing by the kitchen door.

Our daughter Moriah and a neighbor boy had fallen through the ice on the Rehoboth pond, just half a mile from our house. In their heavy winter jackets and thick boots, they plunged into bitter-cold January water, deep enough to cover their heads. They frantically treaded water until the boy's cousin was able to pull them across the ice and into the frozen reeds.

Later, as darkness crowded out the day, Tim and I found ourselves huddled together on the living room couch. We bundled Moriah in a blanket and stroked her hair, still damp from a warm soak in the tub. Ian and his brother, Tyler, leaned heavy against us. Without saying anything, Tim and I both knew that the day could have ended differently. We knew that kids can panic in cold water. That waterlogged boots and clothes can sink a child like a stone. That ice doesn't always hold rescuers. And yes, we also knew that while God protected Moriah and her friend that day, many devoted parents and grandparents pray for protection and come away grieving. Some of you are still healing from agonies like that. Some of you are dreading them. If so, you know better than most that when tragedies and traumas occur, fear can enter our hearts before faith has a chance to slam the door.

Is there an event in your life or in your children's lives that shook you to the core? That stripped away your confidence in a "protected existence"? That made room for fear to incubate in your heart? What was it?

Can you trace how that event has affected you? Changed you? Are there dangers you vigilantly protect your kids or yourself against because of it? A new level of trust you found?

How have you made sense (or are you making sense) of God's involvement in the event and its aftermath? What are your thoughts about His role in it?

Digging In

Fear affects us all. On the positive side, God uses fear to help us detect and avoid dangerous or harmful situations. Thanks to appropriate fear, we don't bungee-jump without double-checking the cord (or maybe we don't bungee-jump at all!). We don't drink bleach, swim in riptides, or ride bikes in lightning storms, and we don't let our children do those things either. These cautions literally safeguard our lives by keeping us from harm, and they reflect God's wisdom and love for us.

However, fear is also a product of the fall. It's woven into Eden's curse to prevent us from doing what matters most in life: loving God and others. The antidote for it, while certainly a process, is quite simple: we must abandon ourselves to the love of God. John, Christ's disciple, taught that if we want fear to diminish in our lives, we must seek Christ's love. Listen to this: "There is no fear in love. But perfect love drives out fear. . . . We love because He first loved us" (1 John 4:18, 19).

But there's the sticking point. Even though God's love is perfect, for many of us it hasn't always felt safe, secure, or reliable. If we just knew God would keep us safe, why, we'd trust Him in a minute with our children and our lives. But He hasn't always done that. We've miscarried, lost mothers in our youth, seen grown sons sent to jail, sat through chemotherapy with two-year-olds, and raised children scarred by horrible accidents. And even if we haven't, we know we could have or still might.

And so as authors Brent Curtis and John Eldredge so powerfully point out, we must decide whether to trust in "The Sacred Romance," in a heroic but unpredictable love story between us and God that will ultimately end beautifully and well, or "The Message of the Arrows," a smaller plot, focused on the things that have deeply wounded us and our children (and on ways to avoid those wounds in the future).[1]

The choice is ours: "Should we keep our hearts open to the Romance [to love and promise] or concentrate on protecting ourselves from the Arrows [from adversity and struggle]? Should we live with hopeful abandon . . . or . . . glean what we can from the Romance while trying to avoid the Arrows?"[2]

Listen to how love and fear differ in the words of Jay Adams, and decide which one you want to offer the kids in your life: "Love looks for opportunities to give; it asks 'What can I do for another?' Fear keeps a wary eye on the possible consequences of involvement and asks: 'What will he do to me?' Love 'thinks no evil'; fear thinks of little else. Love 'believes all things'; fear is highly suspicious. Love is so busy doing today's tasks that it has no time to worry about tomorrow. Because it focuses upon tomorrow, fear fails to undertake responsibilities today. Love leads to greater love. . . . Fear, in turn, occasions greater fear."[3]

Clearly, At-Promise relationships need to be grounded in love instead of fear. The teaching, practical applications, reflections, and questions presented in the remainder of this workbook will walk you, step by step, through a courageous and loving adventure with the kids in your care. And they will help you believe that we are not abandoned when we go through trials but are supported and loved by a fearless God who knows what it takes to shape our promise. A safe, small existence is less than God intends for us and our children. He wants us to set out on a risk-laden but sovereign journey with Him, courageously embracing His unknown will and enjoying a love so profound that our safety becomes secondary to the promise that awaits us. Without a doubt, such a prospect can leave us with pounding hearts; however, the alternative is to protect our hearts altogether until we shrink from the risk of loving and being loved.

If you are disillusioned with your efforts to stir up human love, if you know how powerless you are to defeat fear by focusing on it, move in another direction. Ask God to give you a convincing experience of His love. Really. Ask Him. We can only love fearlessly because He first loves us.

Barriers and Breakthroughs

Do you consider yourself a fearful person? Why or why not?

Fear can go undetected as it flows beneath the surface of our lives, but it has real consequences. "Fear can mutate, prevent, or restrict our intimacies, choices of spouses, educational decisions, careers, parenting styles, hobbies, health, personalities, life expectancies—pretty much everything" (*Children At Promise*, p. 34). Looking over this list, what choices in your life have you made (or avoided) because of fear? For example, did you choose a "safe" college major instead of pursuing your passion? Did you avoid college altogether because you feared you "didn't have the brains"? Do you swallow your opinions so you won't be misunderstood or rejected? Do you err on the side of leniency with your kids to avoid conflict? Are you rigidly inflexible with your kids to avoid unpredictable outcomes? Have you passed up new career opportunities because you're afraid of change? Have you avoided relationships for fear of rejection?

Do you coach your kids or students to make similar fear-based decisions? Do you counsel them to avoid risk even when they want to take on appropriate challenges? Why?

When we see our fears in black and white, we begin to know where God's love needs to transform us. On page 33 of *Children At Promise* you were asked to list your deepest fears about kids (either your own kids or those you love or work with). What are those fears? What are you afraid might happen to your children? What do you fear they might do or become? Answer courageously.

Are you afraid that you will negatively affect your kids in some way or that they will negatively affect you? Do you fear the impact you've already had on your kids? Why? What's been going on?

Do you appeal to fear in your discipline of children? Do you use anger, intimidation, punishments, and threats to move kids toward submission? If so, how do your children respond?

Pages 39–42 of *Children At Promise* identify four distinguishing traits of fear: control, denial, isolation, and hopelessness. Examining these symptoms will help you identify how fear affects your lifestyle and relationships. Let's look at those traits again:

- Control—restraining, regimenting, or rigidly orchestrating the lives of others
- Denial—refusing to acknowledge, admit, or tell the truth to ourselves and others
- Isolation—seeking distance from others, avoiding closeness, resisting intimacy
- Hopelessness—expecting the worst, giving up on solutions, despairing

Which of these traits do you struggle with most? In what ways?

Thankfully, as love drives fear from our lives, four opposite traits begin to emerge:

- Flexibility—openness to differences and change
- Honesty—openness to the truth (about ourselves, God, and others)
- Connection—openness to being known and knowing others
- Hope—openness to blessing, positive change, and solutions

Which of these traits comes most naturally to you? How do you express them with your children, grandchildren, or students?

Striking the Flint

"Listen to me . . . all you whom I have upheld since you were conceived, and have carried since your birth. Even to your old age and gray hairs, I am he, I am he who will sustain you. I have made you and I will carry you; I will sustain you and I will rescue you. To whom will you liken me that we may be compared? . . . Remember this, fix it in mind, take it to heart. . . . I am God, and there is none like me. I make known the end from the beginning, from ancient times, what is still to come" (Isaiah 46:3–5a, 8–9).

Cutting to the Chase:
A Frequently Asked Question

When is control appropriate and love-based, and when is it fear-based?
The early years of any child's life are often characterized by much appropriate, love-based control. Parents simply have to make decisions for kids who are too young to make those decisions themselves. A child's choice of clothing, food, entertainment, and even friendships in this stage is often dictated by the parent. However, be careful of doing for your children what they can do for themselves, especially if you're motivated to take over out of fear. The early training a parent offers should lead children

to greater independence and self-direction, not less. Some parents have difficulty letting their children grow up because their kids' dependence makes them feel useful. Others control their children's choices and decisions for fear that their kids will make costly, embarrassing, or immoral choices without their intervention. Ultimately, we want our children to be directed by the Holy Spirit and not controlled by us. If we use fear to control them, they will not get used to hearing the Spirit's voice because God doesn't move us through a spirit of fear but through power, love, and a sound mind (2 Timothy 1:7).

Observation Guide

In each chapter of this book, we will ask you in this section, to observe yourself and your children in a given area for a week. As you do, use your personal Observation Journal to record your insights and to answer the guided questions we pose. To maintain your focus, we encourage you to read the observation questions or assignments several times during the week, perhaps at night or in the morning, so you can reflect on and prepare for the day's focal point. Of course, your best insights and observations on a given topic may surface at any time. That's why we encourage you to make an ongoing habit of recording your observations. Whenever new discoveries surface, feel free to capture them in your Observation Journal.

This first Observation Guide is longer than most. From it, though, you'll identify just one symptom of fear (out of four) that you struggle with most: control, denial, isolation, or hopelessness. After reading the entire guide, choose one symptom to focus on and then observe how it manifests itself in your life and with your kids in the coming week. (Of course, if you want to observe more than one area, that's fine too.)

Control Versus Flexibility

This week, watch for ways you may be trying to control others in your home or at work. In what areas are you most inflexible? How is your spirit affected by your efforts to direct circumstances, people, or outcomes? How are your children affected? Are you achieving the results you're seeking? And what are you afraid will go wrong if you just let events unfold without your direction?

"When we let love drive out our fear, we gradually decrease our controlling behavior. We realize that we are not fatherless; God . . . loves us and will act in our very best interests if we will just trust Him. He has a plan for all those circumstances and people we are trying to manipulate" (*Children At Promise*, p. 43).

Denial Versus Honesty

Fearful thoughts can keep us from getting involved when we're needed most. This week, watch for warning signs, question marks, or revelations about your child's behavior, character, or relationships that require your interest and attention. What are they? Have you been avoiding issues that need to be addressed or discussed with your child? Which ones? Have you been avoiding issues that need addressing in your own life? What are they?

"Love allows us to be honest—and courageous. We don't have to deny and blame anymore. We don't have to hide from each other. We no longer need to run and protect ourselves at others' expense. No matter how badly we have messed up with our kids, we can come to God and find a fresh start. . . . We can acknowledge our own mistakes. . . . We can apologize. We can talk directly about difficult issues without feeling threatened" (*Children At Promise*, pp. 43–44).

Isolation Versus Connection

This week, notice situations or people you avoid out of fear. What do you fear might be revealed or might happen if you get involved? How do you feel about choosing isolation over connection? Relieved? Guilty? Anxious? Also notice whether you gravitate to people who are equally or more uncomfortable with intimacy as you are. This pattern can serve as a fearful protection from getting too close to others.

"Love connects us. Where fear once isolated us, the safe, pure love that comes from God allows us to develop deep, trusting relationships with friends, spouses, relatives, and children we care about" (*Children At Promise*, p. 44).

Hopelessness Versus Hope

Fear diminishes and lessens hope. Have you decided that even God can't transform certain circumstances in your life? What are they? Are you skeptical or even numb when others suggest strategies or solutions for parenting or teaching? Consider throughout the week whether you spend more time focusing on hopeless circumstances or on hopeful possibilities. Remember, moving from fear to love requires lifting our eyes from the seen (the hard facts of our lives) to the unseen (God's ability to make all things new).

"Love gives us hope. No matter how grim a report our eyes and ears may give us about our kids, we believe God, who tells us that He is 'able to do immeasurably more than all we ask or imagine, according to his power that is at work within us' (Ephesians 3:20). . . . I stake my life—and the lives of the children I care about—on the fact that 'nothing is impossible with God'" (Luke 1:37) (*Children At Promise,* pp. 44–45).

A Prayer of Surrender

The truth is, God doesn't deliver us from fear by banishing all trouble, risk, pain, and disappointment from our lives. God delivers us from fear when we abandon our lives and plans into His care, trusting that His love will sustain us through everything. As we move toward this abandoned life, we can pray along with Thomas Merton:

> My Lord God, I have no idea where I am going. I do not see the road ahead of me. I cannot know for certain where it will end. . . . But I believe that the desire to please you does in fact please you. And I hope I have that desire in all that I am doing. . . . Therefore I will trust you always though I may seem to be lost and in the shadow of death. I will not fear, for you are ever with me, and you will never leave me to face my perils alone.[4]

CHAPTER 4

Companions for the Journey

Choosing Your At-Promise Kids

You did not choose me, but I chose you.

—John 15:16

Here's the fun part. On the following page you'll find space to identify and honor the At-Promise kids in your life. These are the kids you'll be thinking about as you work through Chapters Five through Thirteen of the workbook. Dedicate the first section to family members and the second section to other At-Promise children in your life.

Start by writing the names of your own children (and grandchildren, if you have them). You may want to paste snapshots or draw pictures of each one. Beside each name, express the qualities and future promise you see in the kids you've listed. You may want to journal, doodle, flowchart, mind-map, or simply list these qualities. (If you struggle to see the promise in one or more of your children, this exercise may be more difficult for you. It's OK to leave an empty space beside a name or two. If you do, though, turn that vacant spot into a prayer. Ask God to give you insight so you can return to this page with specific affirmations He will reveal to you about each of your children.)

Family Members

Now branch out. Think of the kids in your neighborhood, classroom, team, extended family, church, or other organization or group to which you belong. Are there specific children whose promise jumps out at you? Is there a child who's been seeking your friendship or whose nature and companionship delights you? Have you felt burdened for or been drawn to help a particular child in need? Is there a child in your extended family or a student whom you "love like your own"? These kids could very well be a part of your extended At-Promise family. List their names and describe either what you see in them or why they're calling you to connect with them. (This list will change over time and may be different today than it was a year ago.) Who are your current At-Promise kids?

Other Children

TWO

Requirements for Growth

Maybe you've seen Pixar's blockbuster film Finding Nemo with your kids or grandkids. In it we meet Marlin, a bereaved and overprotective clownfish who loses his wife and unhatched children in a nasty shark attack. In his anguish, Marlin makes a vow to his only surviving son, Nemo, saying, "Daddy's here and I promise—I will never let anything happen to you." Marlin's promise, we discover, is as much for himself as it is for Nemo. He can't possibly bear another traumatic loss in his life and is suddenly terrified by the ominous ocean that drops off outside his cozy anemone.

Friendless and alone, Marlin clamps down on Nemo. He encourages him to "play on the sponge beds" and to "hold his fin" when crossing the ocean. He drills Nemo, asking, "What's the one thing you have to remember about the ocean?" Nemo answers, "It's not safe." "That's right," Marlin says.

Eventually, Nemo rebels against Marlin's restrictions and fears. He defies his dad by swimming past the ocean's dropoff and is captured in a diver's net. Nemo lands helpless (but surrounded by new friends) in a dentist's aquarium on the edge of Sydney Harbor. What follows is a wise, at times hysterically funny, and moving depiction of Marlin and Nemo's heroic journey out of the territory of fear and into the uncharted waters of risk and love.

To prepare for Chapters Four, Five, and Six, we recommend that you watch and discuss Finding Nemo *with your Breakfast Club, with your family, or by yourself. Even if you've seen it more than once, chances are you haven't watched it from an At-Promise perspective. It's a movie that brilliantly animates just how the surprising gifts of relationship and adversity work together to help us grow—and what it truly means to be "companions for the journey."*

CHAPTER 5

Adversity

What's Pain Got to Do with It?

I know that God won't give me anything I can't handle. I just wish He didn't trust me so much.

—Mother Teresa

But by means of their suffering, he rescues those who suffer. For he gets their attention through adversity.

—Job 36:15

Joy isn't the absence of suffering; it's the presence of God.

—Unknown

Getting Ready

We're heading into a stage of the journey that requires the most stamina and courage. Though this chapter is not very long, it will likely take you weeks or months to fully test, confirm, and embrace the concepts presented here. No matter how long it takes, though, we challenge you to grapple unflinchingly with your assumptions about adversity's place in your children's lives. Whether your child has battled overwhelming trials or been deliberately protected from them, the quest remains equally demanding.

Before you work through this chapter, take time to read or reconsider Chapter Four in *Children At Promise*, "Adversity and Pain Can Lead to Growth."

Connecting

What ideas struck you as you read or reviewed the Adversity chapter? What questions or thoughts did it inspire? Record those here.

Real Life: Where the Journey Begins

Two mothers enrolled their firstborn three-year-olds in swimming lessons one summer. Neither of the children took to the water eagerly. They cried, spluttered, and stiffened in fear—all to be expected from preschool tadpoles. However, while one mother found it easier to trust the instructor, it soon became obvious that the other mother couldn't stand to see her child struggle. She was like a caged bear in the glassed-in viewing room. She blurted, "Why isn't the teacher making sure Gina's ready before putting her face underwater?" and "Look at how the teacher is letting her get water in her mouth!" The mother could hardly restrain herself from jumping in the pool and taking over the class herself.

A big blow came weeks later when Gina wasn't promoted to the intermediate class while her sidekick was. Gina's father, a charming and successful businessman, picked up his daughter that afternoon and received the disappointing news. In a spontaneous attempt to reverse the decision, he used his well-honed negotiation skills at the side of the pool with the instructor.

Trail Warnings

For the sake of clarity, we discuss adversity and trusting relationship in separate chapters in the workbook, but be sure to fuse them together in your mind. Ideally, we want to raise children in an atmosphere where both adversity and trusting relationship exist in healthy proportions.

Allowing children to go through adversity and hardship alone is not consistent with the At-Promise philosophy. Neither is inflicting any kind of intentional harm, cruelty, or abuse on kids. In other words, the At-Promise approach is not advocating that adults load kids up with painful experiences so that they can learn to endure suffering. It does advocate, however, that parents and mentors learn to see each natural struggle that a child bears as a potential gift not only for the child but for *everyone who bears it together.*

"Ah, listen, isn't there something we can do to pass my daughter to the next level?" he ventured. "Couldn't she just catch up in the intermediate class? After all, do you seriously fail kids in beginners? Isn't that a bit harsh?"

This story reveals something that most of us know only too keenly: how brutal it can be to see our kids struggle and fail. It also underscores our temptation to advance our kids beyond their depth for the sake of salving our own insecurities and fears. Without a doubt, three-year-old Gina was oblivious to the notions of passing, failing, and (early onset) upward mobility. It's highly unlikely that repeating beginner swimming lessons would damage her self-esteem or stigmatize her as an underachiever. In reality her "failure" made little difference to her at all—but boy, was it painful for her parents to accept!

Digging In

Without thinking about it, many of us assume that the following equation is true:

Children + (emotional protection + financial provision + enrichment opportunities) − (hardship and adversity) = success

In other words, children will inherit a bright future if we help them bypass struggle and we offer them tons of provision and protection. In general, we see adversity, loss, and hardship as the enemies of our children's promise and try to avoid them at all cost.

For anyone holding these assumptions, though, the At-Promise perspective introduces some pretty tough statements. Chew on these from *Children At Promise* for a while:

"Pain is absolutely essential to building successful individuals" (p. 51).

"Children who have not experienced adversity are at risk of not reaching their full potential" (p. 52).

"Adversity, in the context of a relationship with a trusted adult, is critical to a child's success in life" (p. 52).

The At-Promise perspective believes that God allows adversity (and orchestrates relationships) not to sabotage our lives but to grow us and to fulfill our promise.

Sometimes adversity outweighs relationship, and sometimes relationship outweighs adversity, but both deposit value in our lives. *Children At Promise* put it this way:

> Picture a child's success like a bank account. To believe that adversity disadvantages a child is to assume that every time a child fails, hurts, or loses, his account balance decreases. Following this logic, the kid with great adversity is left with a severely overdrawn account, with charges and late fees accruing daily. It seems that only a chain of certain successes and positive experiences can reverse the dismal balance.
>
> But what if every time a child experiences pain and adversity, he is making a deposit, not a withdrawal, in his account? What if every time a trusted adult helps him interpret his struggles positively, the balance grows with interest? Then children hurt by family dynamics, overwhelmed with a new language and culture, or trapped by a series of negative choices no longer need to catch up. They are already halfway there.
>
> The At-Promise paradigm, if we take it seriously, can transform the way we counsel, teach, discipline, and mentor the children in our care. If we truly believe that pain and adversity are essential components in a child's positive development, then we no longer need at-risk terminology. All of the factors that traditionally place children at risk are now building blocks of promise. Enfolded by relationship, children's deficits turn into deposits [pp. 66–67].

Scripture makes it clear that while Satan intends adversity to harm us, God intends it for our good. It is a tool to shape us, a surgical instrument to heal us, and sometimes, as C. S. Lewis suggests in *The Problem of Pain*, "a megaphone" to get our attention.[1] In essence, we swindle hope from children, families, schools, neighborhoods, and entire ethnic groups when we look at their adversity as a disease and a deficit in their lives. And we cheat others by convincing them that pain has more power to break them than to make them. We cheat them of the compassion, character, humility, and total abandonment to God's purposes that can be wrought only through adversity.

Barriers and Breakthroughs

So why are we still so resistant to pain? Besides the fact that pain hurts, we all have our personal reasons for dreading it. We promised you ample space to test your assumptions about adversity in this chapter, so now it's your turn to wrestle with those, one on one.

Where do you stand on the need for adversity? Would you say that you're not comfortable with any pain in your child's life (even if it leads to growth), or can you see some good in trials?

What hurtful situations in your kids' lives make you want to rush in to confront or avenge the source of their pain? Think of a specific situation where your child was mistreated or hurt and you took his or her cause into your own hands. What was the result?

Children At Promise makes a critical distinction between "hurt" and "harm" (pp. 60–61). "Hurt is not usually devastating. It causes enough pain to get the attention of the sufferer. . . . Harm, on the other hand, causes serious damage. . . . Confused by where hurt ends and harm begins, we lump the two together, because they both cause pain."

Let's clarify: spraining an ankle, failing to pass twelfth-grade English (a graduation requirement), getting caught shoplifting, or vomiting during the school play exemplifies hurt. Hurt may involve physical, emotional, social, academic, or other pain, but the child's discomfort can be turned to advantage if we don't allow our compassion to paint the child as a victim who cannot recover from it. However, getting raped, being neglected or physically battered, becoming addicted to drugs, or seeing a parent commit suicide exemplifies harm. These experiences violate body, mind, and spirit and have the potential to traumatize and devastate children.

To help you further distinguish between these two forms of adversity, in the following columns list examples of hurt and harm that the kids in your life have experienced.

Hurt   *Harm*

One of the core beliefs expressed in *Children At Promise* is that we need to do all we can to help our kids avoid harm, but "the God who loves us can transform and redeem any misery, no matter how cruel or traumatic or devastating, into something useful and good" (p. 62). Do you believe this? What's your gut response to this statement? Why?

Let's face it: we want our children to "succeed." Even before our kids can walk, we secretly compare the motor skills, alertness, appetite, looks, growth, and "intelligence" of our babies, taking pride in their accomplishments and making worrisome mental notes about their "weaknesses." Later, poor outside evaluations about their behavior, athleticism, or academic promise can strike us like arrows. We desperately want them to do well in life. Unfortunately, our pride can prevent our kids from learning naturally through weakness and stumbling. Are you ever tempted to "improve" on your children's accomplishments or to prevent poor performance by intervening in their activities? How hard is it for you to see your children "outperformed" by others? Why?

When we overprotect our children by steering them away from difficulty, "we are actually doing them a great disservice by expressing our lack of confidence in them—not only in their ability to achieve but in their ability to handle defeat if they don't" (p. 59). Reread this statement and let it soak in for a minute. How confident are you in your child's ability to handle defeat or to achieve?

If we believe that adversity will jeopardize our children's success in life, we will not only protect them from pain but will also protect them from *growth*. Think of a situation where you have protected a child from growth by undermining, reversing, or preventing adversity in his or her life. What happened?

> We need to base our confidence on the fact that God made our kids to be overcomers and offers them His overcoming power. When our kids are in deep trouble, they need to hear us saying, "I believe that you're going to make it through this. I know it seems impossible, but if you lean into God, you can face every aspect of this situation head on. It's not going to be easy—for you or for us—but we're going to walk through it together and somehow come out better for it on the other side."

Think of a time when your child struggled or failed and something good came out of it. What happened, and what were the results (realizations, changes, positive outcomes)?

We can be tempted to fight against, undermine, or overlook the very experiences that have the potential to shape and mature our kids (things as simple as detentions, failing test scores, speeding tickets, accidents, fines, school and community discipline, or broken relationships). However, sometimes we must sacrifice a tidy and respectable short term in order to see our child's character and promise fulfilled in the long term. This continues to be true for parents of adult children who make choices that may deeply grieve them, sometimes over many years.

Striking the Flint

The following reflection is adapted from a call to confession by Rev. Keith Bulthuis of Bethany Christian Reformed Church in Gallup, New Mexico. In it, Keith captures how our trust allows God to shape us through adversity.[2]

Chemically, diamond and coal aren't that dissimilar. Essentially both are carbon. So what destines one to be precisely set by a jeweler in an engagement ring and the other to be shoveled by the cartload into a boiling furnace? In the end, what accounts for their difference in quality, value, and use?

The difference is pressure. And heat.

And what does it take for *us* to become precious jewels? How is it that the Lord looks at you and says, "You shine with all kinds of glory in my eyes"? We're dumbfounded when God says things like that. We blurt back to Him, "I don't see it." And the Lord says, "You will."

How's He going to do it? Pressure. And heat.

When a diamond lies in its original setting, people can sometimes walk by and think it's just another shiny rock, but when it's held in the hands of the master, it gets cut. It has to be painful being cut. But then— it shines with glory.

What does it mean to confess our need for God in our lives? When we confess our need for God's grace, we're confessing that our lives are in God's hands: that these things that happen to us—pressure and heat and cutting—are not just random occurrences but events that take place when we are in the hands of a loving Father who really cares for us. It's hard to say that. But we need that painful action in our lives so that we might become what He's called us to be, that we might enjoy the glory He's prepared for us and that we might reflect His glory. And so when we confess our need for God's grace, we're confessing a lot. We're opening ourselves to a transformation. We're entering into the purpose for which God has called us. And we're trusting Him to change us for the better.

Cutting to the Chase: Frequently Asked Questions

I'm afraid that if I crack the door open to pain in my child's life, something might happen that will cripple instead of strengthen him. How can I be sure that pain will have a positive effect on my child instead of a negative one?

We can't be sure that pain will positively affect each child. Although this answer is not very comforting, I (Tim) don't want to mislead you. Some children are embittered by trials; others are softened by them. It's that simple—and that difficult. Keep in mind, though, that few people welcome trials. That's why the apostle James's teaching to "consider it all joy when [we] encounter trials of various kinds" (James 1:3) is so radical, so important.

However, in my doctoral research, the two factors that were significantly tied to a child's ability to see the benefits of adversity were supportive relationships and personal faith. Teens who ranked these factors the highest in their lives were also the ones who saw the greatest benefits from their adversity. And encouragingly, these two factors were more influential than ethnicity, gender, or the degree of trauma the teen had experienced. So giving kids opportunities to deepen their friendship with both God and supportive mentors can potentially boost their ability to see adversity in a positive light.

Although it may seem too great a risk to let your child experience any degree of adversity, controlling your child's life in order to cushion him from hardship will certainly affect him negatively. At some point he will inevitably have to face pain—only without the navigation tools that could have been developed in a loving relationship at home.

How do you answer critics who say, "Isn't allowing adversity just another way to justify neglect by parents who don't have time to protect their kids?"

The At-Promise philosophy is not neglectful in any way. In fact, it calls parents to face the tough situations their children encounter rather than ignoring or denying them. It combines *high expectations* (kids and adults will work through difficulties and accept trials as a part of life, and together they will grow in PROMISE character through them) with *high support* (adults will love kids and believe in their promise while helping them interpret their struggles).

Am I supposed to fabricate adversity in my kids' lives in order for them to grow?

The wisest and most important form of adversity we can "fabricate" in our kids' lives is loving, consistent, and fair discipline. The Old and New Testaments plead with parents to take discipline seriously because it is a godly means of growth and maturity for children. A child who can learn to deal with "no," face consequences for wrong decisions, accept boundaries, and submit to imperfect authority is on the road to wisdom. As clumsily as we might attempt it, and as hard as it might be to see our kids react and rebel against it, our discipline and our love must be the first "adversity-relationship" experience that our children encounter.

What are other appropriate ways to fabricate adversity to benefit your child? You can encourage your capable teen to tackle tough courses instead of cruising through less demanding ones. You can require your child to do chores, write an apology to a teacher or friend, persevere with piano lessons instead of quitting midyear, take on a summer job to finance his mountain-biking hobby, or play with a neighbor who is ignored on the block. We can also encourage our kids to seize opportunities to serve others.

For the most part, though, plenty of naturally occurring forms of adversity exist for children every day. As parents and mentors, our challenge is to let those difficulties and consequences run their course while we support our kids and help them find perspective. School suspensions, team losses, deaths in the family, and relocations might be examples of these. We don't move from Southern California to North Dakota just to shake things up a bit for our kids, but when our job is transferred, our supportive role is suddenly made clear for us in the transition.

Assessing Adversity

Now comes the first of nine At-Promise assessments your kids will complete, with or without your help, during the course of this workbook. After completing each assessment, record your child's score in the At-Promise Profile at the back of the book. Together, the nine scores will give each participant an overview of his or her AT-PROMISE strengths and weaknesses. The table is set up to hold the assessment scores of four participants; you may use your own similar table to record the scores of additional participants. These scores are not meant to "label" kids in any given area. They simply represent a starting point for growth, and over time, they can help you see the progress your At-Promise kids are making. After each assessment, we offer relationship-centered pointers to help your kids grow stronger in their weak areas. Have fun!

Note that the statements in each survey are written so that your child (ages nine to eighteen) can read them and answer them independently. If your child is eight or younger, you may want to read the questions to the child out loud or complete the survey yourself, based on what you have observed to be true about your child's experience.

Please have your At-Promise kids complete Worksheet 5.1 now.

Assessing Adversity

Think about the most difficult event you have experienced in the past two years. Identify that event here:

Indicate whether the following statements describe the outcome of your difficult event by circling the appropriate answer.[3]

1. As a result of this event, I am more sensitive to the needs of others.   Yes   No

2. Because of this event, I have a greater faith in God.   Yes   No

3. Because of this event, I am more sensitive to people in similar situations.   Yes   No

4. This event taught me that I can handle most things.   Yes   No

5. As a result of this event, I learned that my family loves me.   Yes   No

6. Because of this event, I am more aware of how much my family means to me.   Yes   No

7. I am a more effective person because of what I went through.   Yes   No

8. Because of this event, I have developed new friends.   Yes   No

9. This event made me a stronger person.   Yes   No

10. Because of this event, I am a more capable person.   Yes   No

Worksheet 5.1.

Scoring: Simply add up the "Yes" answers to determine your child's score. Record this score in the At-Promise Profile at the back of the book (p. 157).

For the event identified, a score of 6 or more suggests that your child clearly perceives that negative experiences can yield positive results. A score of 3 to 5 suggests a growing ability to perceive the benefits of adversity, and a score of 0 to 2 suggests a weak ability to see advantages in adverse circumstances.

Why is this ability important? Research shows that individuals who are able to perceive the benefits of adversity are more likely to recover from, overcome, and even grow positively from the traumatic and painful events they encounter.[4] In other words, the first step to experiencing the benefits of adversity is to perceive that benefits exist in the first place.

Growing Stronger Through Relationships

Relationally, we need to remember that kids are better equipped to see the benefits of adversity if we help them interpret the pain they experience. But how do we help them do that without becoming an on-call Confucius? Here are a few tips:

Listen, listen, and listen. An interpreter who doesn't hear (or want to hear) a child's message will not bring understanding.

Admit that some things don't make sense even after much time has passed.

Offer your presence more than your brilliance. Beware of too many words.

Empathize. The old saying holds true, especially for kids: they don't care what you know until they know that you care. Are you moved by their struggles or immune to them?

Pray for wisdom. God gives it ungrudgingly to everyone who asks. Ask!

Change your mind-set about suffering. Your core beliefs about pain and adversity are far more important than anything you will ever say to your kids. If you fear adversity, you will either avoid the topic altogether or communicate dread and disaster when you face it. However, if you believe that treasure can be born through adversity, you will anticipate blessing and communicate courage. Which approach is the better gift to your child?

Here's how your actions and attitudes interpret adversity to kids:

Your *presence* says, "You're not alone."

Your *optimism* and *hope* say, "You're life's not ruined. You're going to make it."

Your *belief in God's control and wisdom* says, "Each trial has meaning and purpose. You're not the victim of random, cruel circumstances."

Your *openness* says, "Pain isn't always an enemy. I'm willing to be shaped by it. How about you?"

Your *focus on promises rather than circumstances* says, "Big problems are never bigger than God's purposes. Let's figure out how to trust Him, even in this situation."

What do you think your actions and attitudes communicate to your kids about adversity?

Observation Guide

Over the next week, use the following ideas and questions to guide you as you observe how you and your kids *truly* face adversity. You can jot quick notes as you read through this section, but use your personal Observation Journal to record or expand your thoughts.

1. Observe and record the natural struggles your children encounter in the coming week. How does each child respond uniquely to trials?

2. Consider your reaction to your children's adversity. What do you feel, say, or do when your kids are in trouble (hurt, sick, confused, disciplined)? What are some of your standard lines and reactions? In the long run, do you think your reactions build bridges or barricades between you and your kids? Do your reactions paint adversity as a friend or a foe?

3. Watch how you respond when difficult situations come up for you at work, in a friendship, at church, or elsewhere. What do your reactions teach your kids about facing tough times? Do you see those situations as "training" or as traumatic?

4. Are you allowing your children to experience adversity through consequences? Are they allowed to experience the full extent of those consequences, or are they usually "let off the hook"? Is one child in particular (or one student, if you're a teacher or mentor) more prone to getting released from consequences than the others? If so, why?

5. When you intervene in a child's struggle, continue to ask yourself this question: "If I cut off this struggle, am I protecting this child from harm (out of love), or am I protecting this child from growth (out of fear)?"

A Prayer for Hurting Parents

Lord, when pressure and heat are applied to our lives and our children's lives, it feels like we are about to be consumed, not transformed. When our children are cut, it feels as if they will bleed to death, not be changed into something glittering bright and glorious. When, together, we are going through the darkness of life, we are not always sure there is light on the other side. But we come here to tell you that we want to believe. Help us in our unbelief. Lord, we place ourselves in your hands—asking you to be gentle, loving, and restoring: giving us the glory that you promised us. We pray this because of Jesus, who went through the pressure, the cutting, and the heat of the cross. Amen.[5]

CHAPTER 6

Trusting Relationships with At-Promise Kids

Every act of love is a risk of the self.

—Eugene Peterson

Do not hesitate to love and to love deeply. As you love deeply, the ground of your heart will be broken more and more, but you will rejoice in the abundance of the fruit it will bear.

—Henri J. M. Nouwen

May God help us all to hold a crown before our children and watch them grow into it.

—Randy Roth

Getting Ready

Reflecting on the rocky dynamics between teachers and students at his teaching post in Turkey, Tim wrote me (Mona) a letter saying, "You can't learn from an enemy. You just can't." His understanding that a child's learning and growth are dependent on a trustworthy mentor is central both to the At-Promise perspective and to this chapter. Before digging into the issue more deeply, take time to read or review Chapter Five in *Children At Promise*, "Trust Between a Caring Adult and a Child."

Connecting

What ideas engaged you most as you spent time in the Relationship chapter? Write down the issues, ideas, or unsolved questions you'd like to explore further.

Real Life: Where the Journey Begins

On his way to Scotland in the late 1800s, a British member of Parliament ran his carriage off the road. Mired in mud, the statesman was stranded until a young farm boy arrived to rescue him. Using his team of draft horses, the boy quickly and ably solved the dilemma, pulling the stalled carriage onto solid ground.

Grateful and impressed, the British statesman pressed the boy with payment for his help, but the young man refused the money. He saw his deed as an act of neighborly kindness, nothing more. No need to pay him for that.

Inquiring further, the member of Parliament discovered that this farm boy aspired to be a doctor some day, but the boy doubted his family could afford the education. The statesman seized this opportunity to repay the boy's kindness and offered to contribute to his medical education. And as the years passed, he kept his promise.

Nearly fifty years later, at a tipping point in history, another English statesman battled a deathly case of pneumonia. Winston Churchill's life hung in the balance as Hitler's troops advanced across Europe during World War II. However, thanks to a newly discovered drug called penicillin, Churchill survived.

Penicillin was discovered by the brilliant doctor and researcher Alexander Fleming. As a boy, Fleming once rallied his draft horses to pull a carriage of out of the mud for a statesman in Scotland. That statesman was Sir Randolph Churchill, Winston Churchill's father.

In the words of Howard Dayton, "Randolph Churchill's willingness to help a promising young man reach his potential saved the life of his own son nearly half a century later. And by saving the life of Winston Churchill, indeed, he may have saved all England."[1]

Sir Randolph Churchill, an esteemed and engaged statesman, was neither too important nor too preoccupied to seize upon the promise of a young Scotsman named Alexander Fleming and to act on what he saw. The whole world is blessed for his faith and action.

"An argument broke out among the disciples as to which of them would be the greatest. Jesus, knowing their thoughts, took a little child and had him stand beside him. Then he said to them, 'Whoever welcomes this little child in my name welcomes me; and whoever welcomes me welcomes the one who sent me. For he who is least among you all—he is the greatest'" (Luke 9:46–50).

Digging In: A Cheat Sheet for At-Promise Relationships

As a high school principal, it thrills me (Tim) to offer you a legitimate, bona fide "cheat sheet" on At-Promise relationships. Feel free to scrawl the following ideas on your palms or write them on your sleeve if that's what it takes to remember them. Once you capture what At-Promise relationships look like, you'll be more likely to spot them and initiate them. *Grace* and *growth* are the two common denominators you'll see in every one of the following points. Let's take a look.

What At-Promise Relationships Are

- *Free of charge.* They don't begin with reference checks and end with billing statements. Through them, we experience God's favor and covenant love and pass them on to kids as a *gift:* unearned, nonrepayable, full of grace and generosity.

- *Trustworthy.* Kids heal when surrounded by trusting, authentic, honest relationships. Fickle relationships only add to their adversity.

- *A calling.* Callings can be accepted or rejected, but At-Promise thinkers anticipate being summoned, appointed, and used to affirm the promise in kids. It's a part of our life description. As parents, our primary calling is to forge At-Promise relationships with our own children over a lifetime. But God will point out other children and show us their promise as well. In those cases, our calling may be sparked by compassion, interest, faith, circumstance, or obedience.

- *Interpreters of adversity.* Adults interpret the meaning of trials to kids in a way that inspires perseverance, hope, and an overcoming spirit.

- *Based on action and character (not assets and deficits).* At-Promise relationships call us to notice, love, and pray for children; to grow and change; to struggle; to stick with our kids through all the stages of life; to hold our kids accountable for their actions; to be optimistic about their future (and ours!); to offer them a picture of their true identity; to do the right thing even when it hurts; to contribute through serving others; and to play, play, play! More than philosophical, these relationships depend on action.

- *Imperfect.* Don't confuse At-Promise relationships with "idyllic" relationships. At some point, we're destined to mess up, throw a wrench in a child's "actualization," or saddle our kids with unwanted baggage. And it works both ways. Kids routinely (and necessarily) alter adult plans for a perfect life. Imperfection is not unfortunate. When children see us handle our imperfections with humility, they gain the courage to be authentic.

- *Transformational.* At-Promise relationships challenge and change kids and adults because true love always transforms.

- *Not time-bound.* At-Promise relationships depend on God's blueprint and His workmanship in kids' lives, not on our strategies and formulas. Through these relationships, we learn to prize process and faithfulness instead of trying to force God's hand to meet *our* objectives for our children on *our* timetable.

Obviously, At-Promise relationships do not create perfect families or perfect children. They equip and support kids to face all of life—the bumps and the glory—trusting that absolutely everything can contribute to the fulfillment of God's perfect purposes in their lives.

Barriers and Breakthroughs

As you look through the "cheat sheet" we've just presented, figure out which is the hardest point for you to act on. Can you explain why?

Sometimes "busyness" can limit our relationships with kids. In what ways do you feel too busy or preoccupied to connect with your own or other people's kids?

Does "slowing down" provide relief in your relationships, or does it highlight other issues in your family (tensions, inadequacies, lack of true interest, unsolved discipline problems) that you need to address? What issues?

It's funny how few of us claim to be parenting experts beyond the inaugural year of our firstborn's life. At our lowest points, we may even wonder whether our kids are better off with other people (coaches, teachers, neighbors) who are "gifted professionals," who "have a knack with children," or who can give them what we lack. Despite the fact that our parenting is best complemented by the love and interest of other adults, "studies have shown that high school students name their parents as the most 'significant' adults in their lives."[2] Do you think you understand the value and significance you have to your children? How confident are you that your opinions, example, and influence are vital to them? What makes you think so?

Have you seen the glaring promise in a certain child only to realize later that what you saw wasn't obvious to others? In which child? How did you respond to the vision you'd been given? Did you act on it in any way?

Apart from certain types of adoption, we generally don't choose our children. God determines which little ones will land in our bassinettes. Though hard to admit, keeping our own children's promise in focus can sometimes be harder than finding it in others. Do you struggle to see the promise in one or more of your kids? What factors get in the way (behaviors, words, attitudes, circumstances, habits)?

Do certain glimpses of faith about your child or about God's ways help you in your struggle to believe in his or her promise? If so, what are they?

What characteristics distract you from seeing promise in other people's kids?

We all know that kids can "burn" us. As counselors, teachers, parents, coaches, or others who care about kids, most of us eventually bear scars inflicted by kids we trusted, loved, and invested in. Have you ever had a relationship with a child blow up in your face? What happened? How does that experience make you feel about investing in kids today?

Look back at the "cheat sheet" for At-Promise relationships. Jot down all the ways that At-Promise relationships reflect "the ultimate relationship," our relationship with God.

Now think about how a child's relationship with God can surpass an At-Promise relationship. What does God offer kids that a caring adult never can?

Our heroic aspirations can tempt us to see ourselves as the sole answer to a child's problems; we may even try to single-handedly turn a life or two around. But we must remember that we are not the source of love, only reflections of it. As soon as we think we are the healers, life-changers, and promise-fulfillers, we will not just frustrate ourselves—we will fail. Our hope is that kids will acquire a taste for God's love, not be satisfied with imitations. The promise we call out in kids is sealed and fulfilled by God alone: Christ in them, their hope of glory.

Striking the Flint

In *Children At Promise,* Tim and Cheryl describe how God can give each of us a vision of a certain child's promise: a vision that is so clear, it's like an image emerging from one of those Magic Eye art books. Once we see it, we can never "unsee" it, though it may remain a confounding mystery to others. Eugene Peterson captures the essence of how promise eyesight works in his own beautiful prose:

> Love opens eyes. Love enables the eyes to see what has been there all along but was overlooked in haste or indifference. Love corrects astigmatism so that what was distorted in selfishness is now perceived accurately and appreciatively. Love cures shortsightedness so that the blur of the distant other is now in wondrous focus. Love cures farsightedness so that opportunities for intimacy are no longer blurred threats but blessed invitations. Love looks at [Christ] who had no "form or comeliness that we should look at him, and no beauty that we should desire him" and sees there the "fairest of the sons of men . . . anointed with the oil of gladness above your fellows" (Isaiah 51).
>
> If we could see the other as he is, as she is, there is no one we would not see as "fairest . . . all fragrant with myrrh and aloes and cassia" (Psalm 45). Love penetrates our defenses that have been built up to protect against rejection and scorn and belittlement, and it sees life created by God for love. When we look through eyes diseased by self-love, we see neither beauty nor virtue. We stumble in a blurred, unfocused, misshapen world and complain that it is ugly or threatening or boring.[3]

Cutting to the Chase:
Frequently Asked Questions

What should I look for in people who coach, teach, or work with young people? How can I "screen for relationships" in the youth programs I'm considering for my kids?
   Whether you're choosing a program for your own kids or hiring individuals to work with youth, look for people who possess what we call the "five C's":

1. The ability and desire to *connect* with kids.

2. Evidence of PROMISE *character.* (If you're hiring, you can include interview

questions that assess the strength of PROMISE character traits or look for these traits in reference letters.)

3. *Competence.* Kids need skilled mentors, not just "nice" ones.

4. *Compassion.* Truly caring and empathetic individuals help kids experience love and believe in their lovability.

5. *Courage* to hold kids accountable and to help them grow through difficulty.

Although the "five C's" may be difficult to detect in a first meeting with program staff or potential hires, listen carefully to what they say in interview answers, program overviews, or orientation talks. Do they emphasize schedules, credentials, program structure, and reputation while ignoring staff attributes, kids' needs, and the value of relationships? Do they combine supportive relationships with high expectations (accountability)? Do they express hope for all kids? Do they understand that ultimately, caring adults are the gift, the inspiration, the transformational factor in kids' lives regardless of how "successful" or "dynamic" the program is? Finally, look for individuals that you would like your children to know and be influenced by. If you come up empty, continue your search.

What signs indicate that a relationship between an adult and a child is inappropriate?
Whenever an adult puts self-gratification before the best interests of a child, something is wrong. Unfortunately, children can be used to fill the empty places in an adult's life (becoming a substitute for a lost or "distant" spouse, a trophy to bolster a parent's self-esteem, or a scapegoat to blame for a parent's problems). In other cases, the child is ignored for the sake of the adult's own convenience. Such self-centeredness can evolve to a harmful point where a child is neglected, injured, or abused as a result. Then the relationship must be altered radically or cut off. Sexually molesting or physically or verbally abusing children is inexcusable. Adults bear the responsibility to provide *other-centered* relationships; these are the *only* kind of healthy relationships between adults and children.

Assessing Relationships

Worksheet 6.1 gives you an indication of how well supported your child feels.[4] Please have your child complete the worksheet now. (As noted in Chapter Five, if your child is eight or younger, you may want to read the questions aloud or complete the survey on your child's behalf.)

Assessing Relationships

1. I get along with my parents.   Yes   No

2. My parents often tell me they love me.   Yes   No

3. In my neighborhood, a lot of people care about me.   Yes   No

4. My teachers really care about me.   Yes   No

5. I get a lot of encouragement at my school.   Yes   No

6. My parents often ask me about my homework.   Yes   No

7. My friends give me help and support when I need it.   Yes   No

8. I look forward to spending time with adults.   Yes   No

9. If I have an important concern about friendships, teachers, or some other serious issue, I would talk to an adult about it.   Yes   No

10. There are people who encourage me whenever they see me.   Yes   No

Worksheet 6.1.

Scoring: Add up the "Yes" answers to determine each child's score. Record this score in the At-Promise Profile at the back of the book. A score of 6 or more suggests that a child feels strongly supported in his or her relationships. A score of 3 to 5 suggests that a child feels moderately supported by others. A score of 0 to 2 suggests that your child does not feel strongly supported by the people around him or her.

Why is this important? Resiliency and asset-based educational research suggests that children who possess caring and supportive relationships are more likely to experience academic and social success in life.[5] If your child filled out Worksheet 6.1, it is safe to assume that he or she has a caring and supportive relationship in his or her life. This survey simply allows you to see if your child actually believes that he or she is supported.

Growing Stronger Through Relationships

How do you feel about the level of support your children think they possess in their lives right now? Are you surprised, delighted, concerned? Did their responses match your expectations?

What circumstances or issues do you think might be making your child feel undersupported or strongly supported by caring adults?

If you could do or change anything to offer greater support to your children, what would it be?

Observation Guide

Notice the adults your children meet through your family activities and lifestyle. How comfortable are you with their influence on your kids and the examples they set? Any concerns? Any individuals you'd love your kids to imitate? Who?

In the next few days, strike up a conversation with a child you've never met or with a child you've met but never talked to before. What did you discover about the child? About yourself? Write about your encounter in your Observation Journal.

When you attend an activity, class, or practice with your child in the week ahead, pay attention to how trusting relationships are formed in those circumstances. Do instructors or coaches know your child? Do they call kids by name? Look them in the eye? Treat them with kindness and care? Hold them accountable?

Ask God to show you what He sees in kids, and then be alert for new thoughts or positive insights that cross your mind about the kids you meet. Act on what He shows you.

A Prayer for Vision

Lord, pierce through everything that blinds me to what you see in children. Give me an eye for your workmanship. Even when I don't have a clue how you'll manage to craft your likeness in my kids, keep me from doubting or even despairing because of what I see right now. Where my eyes are "diseased by self love," heal me. Where I am wrapped up in "what I'll get out of this," help me step aside and be wowed by your unexpected blessings. Where I'm jaded, calloused, and timid, Lord break me open so that I can feel the tender love that burns inside you for all children, everywhere. Amen.

THREE

Building PROMISE Character

We want to pause here before walking through the following seven PROMISE character traits—just long enough to get our bearings again. You see, it's easy to charge into a section on character development with an acquisition mind-set: fired up to "be all we can be," motivated to conquer a checklist of attributes, and determined to add these traits to other badges of honor we wear. (If we're honest, we may also be eager to stuff our children full of character as well. After all, we feel so good when they're bursting with qualities we admire.) From an At-Promise perspective, though, we must remember that our development is confirmed by what we contribute, not what we acquire.

Woodrow Wilson understood this distinction. He said this about character: "If you will think about what you ought to do for other people, your character will take care of itself. Character is a by-product, and any man who devotes himself to its cultivation in his own case will become a selfish prig."[1] We love this quote because Wilson tells the truth. Character takes root where self gives way. When we open ourselves up to service and love, we grow in ways that can never be attained by simply concentrating our own "improvement."

The seven PROMISE character traits presented over the next seven chapters ripen in the presence of adversity and trusting relationship. We grow in these areas precisely because we focus on "the other" and allow trials to counsel, instruct, and change us. As adults, we commit ourselves to two things: allowing God to build PROMISE character in us and doing all we can (either by pitching in or standing back) to support God's workmanship in our kids' character. With this in mind, let's move on.

CHAPTER 7

Perseverance
Staying the Course

Perseverance is more than endurance. It is endurance combined with absolute assurance and certainty that what we are looking for is going to happen.

—Oswald Chambers

And let us not grow weary in well-doing, for in due season we shall reap a harvest of blessing, if we do not lose heart.

—Paul to the Galatians (Galatians 6:9)

Just keep swimming. Just keep swimming. Swimming, swimming, swimming . . .

—Dory, in *Finding Nemo*

Getting Ready

The first PROMISE character trait, Perseverance, reminds us that our journey with kids isn't typically an *Around the World in 80 Days* adventure (though it may feel like it at times). Realistically, our journey is more akin to what Eugene Peterson calls "a long obedience in the same direction."[1] To ready yourself for a deeper look at perseverance, read or review Chapter Six of *Children At Promise.*

Connecting

The chapter's statistics about divorce, suicide, and dropout rates, as well as the story of a hopeless HIV patient, express our tendency to lose heart. On the other hand, the accounts of perseverance through illness and loss show how our struggles and the comfort of community can build greater heart in us so we won't give up. What stories or ideas from this chapter moved you, humbled you, or captured your attention? Why?

Real Life: Where the Journey Begins

When I (Mona) was in elementary school, I somehow qualified for a district cross-country meet held on a foggy fall morning at Bear Creek Park. I remember nothing about the meet except that I cried in the parking lot and lied to my friend's mom who drove us there. "I can't run," I pleaded with her. "I'm going to throw up." Likely I *was* nauseated. Surely, I was fearful. The girl who went on to win my event was probably nauseated too. But I didn't know that then. I didn't know that nerves and fears plague competitors. I didn't know that even if I came in last, I would feel better than if I didn't run at all.

I don't recall where I sat while the other girls ran that day. I don't remember having to tell my parents that I scratched the race. All I know is that I got away with quitting. I learned to escape from struggle (and from perseverance) by running away—a pattern that continued into my adult years.

My lesson lost on that Saturday morning became a lesson learned over many years, in many starting gates, in different kinds of races. And though I never ran cross-country again, I like to think of the things I could do and say to inspire my daughter to see a finish line worth crossing if I were in that parking lot with her today.

Can you remember a time when you or your child ran away from a test that seemed too daunting or when you were tempted to bolt but faced a challenge anyway? What happened?

Digging In

Lest you think that perseverance is just a gimmicky word leading off a string of PROMISE character traits, let's look at it more closely. Did you know that the development of every other character trait in a child's life depends on the perseverance the child possesses? Perseverance is the gateway to character because as it grows, it gives kids the stamina to press forward until the character of Christ is formed in them: until they are "mature, complete, not lacking anything" (James 1:4).

Keep in mind, though, that obstacles and perseverance are inseparable. By definition, perseverance is the ability to bear up under trials, to continue though tempted to quit. To persevere is to persist in spite of counterinfluences, opposition, or discouragement. But endless trials alone won't necessarily lead our kids to persevere. As Cheryl says in *Children At Promise,* "Not every irritated oyster produces a pearl, despite its potential" (p. 93). Overwhelmed by an onslaught of trials, kids may be tempted to just give up, to lie down and call it quits—to stop taking their insulin, to quit searching for a true friend, to abandon their college dreams, or to run away from home.

That's why two other supports are required to keep kids in the race. First, the sustaining love of the Holy Spirit and of individuals who breathe enough encouragement and confidence into their lives to keep them moving forward and, second, a vision of a finish line worth crossing. These two things, supportive relationships and goals worth reaching, encourage perseverance in children.

Look closely at a New Testament passage like Romans 5:3–5, and you'll see that kids simply can't learn to persevere unless they struggle: "Suffering produces perseverance; perseverance, character; and character, hope." Perseverance is the bridge that connects suffering and character in kids. The pylons on one end of that bridge rise out of painful experiences. From there, it spans a chasm of discouragement, fear, and defeat to arrive at character on the other side. Try as we might, we can't reach character by any other route. And ultimately, this road leads kids to hope, because having faced tough times, persevered despite temptations to quit, and developed inner strength, kids realize that they can overcome things they once thought impossible to endure.

Unfortunately, many kids never build perseverance, and many parents sabotage its construction. Trouble strikes and kids tumble off a cliff, cursing their suffering as they descend. Parents and teachers look on in horror, ironically blaming adversity for all their problems, not realizing that pain is the launching point to the security and hope they long for their kids to experience.

The difference between At-Promise and at-risk thinking lies in this analogy. At-risk thinking anticipates that kids on the edge of adversity risk plunging into greater trouble. But instead of coming close, teaching kids to scan the horizon for hope, and helping them build a bridge toward it, at-risk thinkers engineer barriers to keep kids from the very pain they need to fulfill their promise. In the process, they inadvertently bar young people from perseverance, character, and hope—all things they need to bear out their calling in life. At-Promise thinking regards difficulty as a foundation on which kids can build the most enduring link to the future God has planned for them: perseverance.

Barriers and Breakthroughs

What are you doing right when it comes to modeling or encouraging perseverance? How are you teaching kids to hang in there and finish the work they've begun?

All of us can love, grow, and hope in spurts. The beauty of perseverance is that it helps us *keep* loving, *keep* growing, and *keep* hoping. What are some areas in your relationship with your kids in which you want to persevere even though your progress may be slow? (Examples might include persevering toward "soft answers" instead of "harsh words," continuing to listen to your child's thoughts even though they conflict with your opinions, or believing that your daughter will trade in her rebellion for a tender and willing spirit one day.)

Do your kids tend to quit on relationships or tasks once they encounter challenges or struggles? What happens to them when trouble strikes? Think of some examples, if you can.

Beware of how your interpretation of events can lead kids to quit. Over the years we've heard parents tell their kids, "If I sat on the bench as much as you, I'd turn in my jersey. Why waste your time?" "We don't have to respect that decision. Let's transfer you out." At the first hint of opposition, which message do your kids hear? "Run!"? "Fight!"? or "Persevere!"?

We live in a quitting culture. We abandon churches, marriages, pregnancies, friendships, schools, associations, ideals, and beliefs—even cable companies and long-distance providers (in exchange for a discount on our first statement). What examples can you think of from your own life, family, or other relationships where quitting won over perseverance? Did it have to?

Do you think a person can succeed without perseverance?

Faith makes perseverance possible because it trains us to believe in unseen rewards, unseen victories, unseen fulfillment. Through it, we learn to continue without immediate gratification or blessing. "Therefore, my dear brothers, stand firm. Let nothing move you. Always give yourselves fully to the work of the Lord, because you know that your labor in the Lord is not in vain" (1 Corinthians 15:58). Jot down your thoughts about how this statement might apply to your perseverance with kids.

Cheryl Bostrom, telling the Seattle half-marathon story in *Children At Promise*, recalls what sustained her running group during months of training: "When we suffered aches and fatigue, we anticipated the joy of completing the race" (p. 97). The runners didn't know exactly what the race's finish would look like, but they relished the thought of it and rehearsed the triumph in their minds. For any of us, kids and adults alike, it's almost impossible to stick with any kind of training without a goal in mind. Do your children have goals? Hopes? Even little ones? What goal are they seeking that is worth facing obstacles and trials to realize?

Now pull a perseverance story out of your family history. It may be an account from your own life, your child's, or another relative's. Jot down some of the details, and then tell the story to your family, a friend, or your Breakfast Club. (If you can, tell how struggle, perseverance, character, and hope factor into the story.)

Striking the Flint

I (Tim), like many of you, saw Mel Gibson's epic film *The Passion of the Christ*. In our local Red Rock Theater with two hundred of my high school students and faculty members, the story laid siege to my throat and my heart. I was a mess. In the midst of Christ's torment, though, I was struck with one characteristic like never before—His perseverance.

Good and evil's ultimate destiny was to be determined at the cross. The fulfillment and completion of Christ's goal could only be accomplished by His ultimate sacrifice. At the same time, Satan's defeat would be sealed at the cross as well—and he knew it. As Christ made His way with the cross on the Via Dolorosa, soldiers, onlookers, and even Satan pounded Him with pain, ridicule, and opposition. Anything to keep Him from finishing His work. Anything to prevent Him from ending His race.

In His lifetime, Jesus often said to others, "My work is not yet done," "My time has not yet come," "My work is not finished." But He took those steps to the cross with such resolve, suffering more than anyone in the history of the world, so that He could ultimately announce to us, "It is finished." You see, perseverance "must finish its work" (James 1:4).

How could Christ endure such agony? What vision kept the staggering and wounded Jesus from abandoning His mission of love? One moment in Gibson's film gives us a glimpse of the "finish line" He saw, of "the joy set before Him." A battered and bloody Jesus, barely able to rise out of the dust after crumbling under the weight of His cross, speaks seven visionary words to His mother. He says, "See, Mother, I make all things new!" Jesus saw beyond the bruising and the scorn to the hope ahead. To Him, hope was not only already fulfilled but visible, and He was walking in the newness of it.

"Let us run with perseverance the race marked out for us. Let us fix our eyes on Jesus, the author and perfecter of our faith, who for the joy set before Him endured the cross, scorning its shame, and sat down at the right hand of the throne of God. Consider Him who endured such opposition . . . so that you will not grow weary and lose heart" (Hebrews 12:1–3).

Are you tempted to give up on anything important right now? Consider the example of Jesus, so you will not lose heart.

Cutting to the Chase: Frequently Asked Questions

Is it ever OK to quit?

It's true that "you gotta know when to hold 'em and know when to fold 'em." Each of us has to listen carefully to our own heart and conscience when deciding whether to pull our kids out of a relationship, activity, or other commitment. But here are some good questions to consider as you do that:

1. Is my child being harmed by this situation? Or am I simply afraid of my child being hurt, disappointed, challenged or uncomfortable?

2. What lesson would my child learn from quitting right now? What legacy does he or she inherit by pulling out? (A sense of justice, righteous protection, and secure boundaries? Or a rescue from responsibility, effort, discipline, and personal investment?)

3. Are my expectations of perseverance age-appropriate, or am I asking too much of my child? If you set out on a six-mile mixed-terrain hike with a two-year-old, don't expect the child to persevere to the end. Along with any expectations for perseverance you must offer your child support. Kids will rebel against perseverance if they're abandoned to stick it out by themselves.

I can't imagine committing myself indefinitely to some of the kids I'm working with. I'm going to completely burn out. How do I persevere through tiring relationships?

First of all, maybe you don't need to commit yourself indefinitely to some of the kids you're working with (unless they're your own!). Perseverance is not a ball and chain. But as a busy parent, I (Mona) have been greatly helped by a simple sentence from Bob Ekblad, a social justice advocate and mentor to Hispanic immigrants, inmates, and residents in Washington State. He says, "Learn to love people in a way that you can love them for the rest of our lives." This statement says to us: love people in a way that makes it possible for you to *keep loving them.* It says to tend to the needs of your own soul: the need for pacing, retreat, recreation, boundaries, Sundays off—whatever it takes to keep loving, keep growing, keep hoping. Unrealistic expectations and a driving pace of investment that you can't sustain will only lead you to abandon kids when you can't keep up with your own agenda. Notice that these boundaries aren't to fortify (buttress, barricade) us *against* relationships but to fortify (rejuvenate, sustain) us *for* relationships.

Assessing Perseverance

Worksheet 7.1 gives you an indication of your child's level of perseverance in the face of adversity. The results should give you a sense of whether perseverance is one of your child's strengths or is an area in need of strengthening.

Have your child complete the worksheet now. (If your child is eight or younger, you may want to read the questions aloud or complete the assessment yourself on your child's behalf.)

Assessing Perseverance

1. When things get hard, I often feel like giving up.   Yes   No

2. I have a hard time finishing what I've started.   Yes   No

3. It is better to give up than to get hurt.   Yes   No

4. I am easily discouraged in the face of challenges.   Yes   No

5. I have a hard time setting goals for myself.   Yes   No

6. My goals are often too hard to reach.   Yes   No

7. I do not like thinking about the future.   Yes   No

8. My friends tell me that I quit too easily.   Yes   No

9. Sometimes I just want to stay in bed to avoid the day.   Yes   No

10. My parents don't make me keep going even when it is hard.   Yes   No

Worksheet 7.1.

Scoring: Simply add up the "No" answers to determine your child's score. Record these results in the At-Promise Profile at the back of the book. A score of 6 or more suggests that your child is well equipped to persevere in the face of adversity. A score of 3 to 5 suggests a growing ability to persevere, and a score of 0 to 2 suggests a tendency to give up when facing challenges.

Growing Strong Through Relationships

Tell "perseverance stories" to your kids. When you hear or read about someone who persevered (or when you do), translate that story into language your kids can understand. The stories we tell communicate the values we prize.

Give your kids a "vocabulary of perseverance." Phrases like "Finish what you started!" and "Stick with it until you're done" or "See it through to the end" will start to guide your children when they're tempted to give up.

Model perseverance. When you're fighting to assemble a bookshelf or a barbecue in front of your kids, give yourself an audible pep talk. Let them hear you say, "I'm going to work on this until I get it figured out" or "I feel like quitting, but I can't wait to see my favorite books lining these shelves. That keeps me going."

Lend a hand. Initial attempts to persevere can be tough on kids. When you see them reaching for the "eject button" to free them from a miserable chore or task, gently come alongside and lend a hand. "Let's get this job finished together."

Observation Guide

What kinds of things can you look for in the next week that will deepen your understanding of your child's perseverance? Begin by watching your child's reactions to snags or obstacles in any activity. Whether opening the milk carton, getting a bike out of the basement, or carrying out a chore, what does your child do with complications? Does he or she immediately turn to you for help? Persist with the task? Look for alternative solutions and try them? Abandon the milk for the orange juice? A *pattern* of always (and quickly) looking for outside intervention might point to some degree of learned helplessness. A *pattern* of persistence and creative problem solving points to growing perseverance. A *pattern* of abandoning tasks in the face of difficulty suggests a lack of stamina and little perseverance.

Two more things to watch for are (1) the level of support you're willing to offer your kids when they are trying new or difficult tasks (don't confuse support with enabling behavior, but remember that it's much harder for your child to learn perseverance without you), and (2) how worthy goals affect your child's perseverance. Kids persevere better when they are working toward a valued goal. Use their goals to keep their eyes fixed on something worth struggling to achieve. (Ultimately, this will help them understand the spiritual perseverance that's described in Hebrews 12, quoted earlier in the chapter.)

Take time to trace your thoughts in your Observation Journal. As you write, new insights will likely emerge as well.

A Prayer for Perseverance

Are you feeling weary? Are you tired of believing good things will result from difficulty—with little to show for your faith? Are you ready to give up in certain areas where the struggle's been long and hard? In the space below, write a prayer that expresses your need for perseverance in a particular area of your life or with your children. Fix your eyes on Him, and let Him strengthen your heart to continue the race set before you. Christ encourages us to persevere in prayer, so don't hesitate to keep knocking, to keep seeking, and to keep hoping. He will answer.

CHAPTER 8

Responsibility for Our Actions

Conquering the Blame Game

No snowflake in an avalanche ever feels responsible.

—Voltaire

Getting Ready

One of my (Tim's) main objectives as a high school principal is to help kids take responsibility for their actions. Students who take responsibility are free and empowered. Students who don't take responsibility for their actions feel bound, powerless, and even victimized. This chapter is dedicated to finding the freedom to own up to our actions, our convictions, and our wrongs and to lead our kids into that freedom too. To make the most of it, quickly scan the prompters in the next section, "Connecting," and then read or review Chapter Seven of *Children At Promise,* "Responsibility for Our Actions."

Connecting

What thoughts and responses did you have to the Responsibility chapter?

I felt . . .

I wondered . . .

I wanted to . . .

Real Life: Where the Journey Begins

Any temptation Tim or I (Mona) might have had to avoid responsibility through self-pity took a serious hit several years ago. In a massive cedar longhouse on the banks of the Pacific Ocean, a seventeen-year-old Lummi Indian girl in a motorized wheel-chair accelerated in spurts across the stage to receive her high school diploma. She was basically a torso—her arms and legs barely six inches long, her body twisted, head arched back, mouth askew. As she crossed the platform, the master of ceremonies read her words of abundant gratitude to her family, her teachers, and her mentors. Without speaking a word, this young woman stunned us with the realization that circumstances do not determine who you become or how you can contribute. One's ability to respond in beauty to life's suffering and opportunity does.

Of all the people in that lodge, this dear girl had reason to consider herself a victim. A severely disabled Native American female, swimming upstream in a world that expected little of her. A classic at-risk poster child. But there she beamed—grateful, accomplished, and steeped in promise fulfilled. All our tattered reasons for not living out our calling lost their power that night. Our young scholar drove back off the stage, and though she seemed too kind and humble to ask it out loud, her laughing, joyful question arose in both Tim's mind and my own. She whispered, "What's keeping you from making the most of the life you've been given?"

Digging In

Let's begin by affirming two basic ideas: successful kids—contributing kids—take responsibility for their actions, and successful parents hold themselves and their children accountable for doing what's right. It's more than OK to expect your kids to own their actions, words, and attitudes—it's *good for them* to do so. It may seem strange that we offer you that assurance, but many parents have become genuinely confused about where their responsibility ends and where their child's begins.

As a teenager, my parents allowed me (Mona) to use their credit card for gas money. I promised (and fully intended) to pay them back at the end of each month. And I did—for the first two months. After that, I didn't pay and they didn't ask. By spring, however, my conscience was killing me. I totaled up my gas bills for the year and wrote a $1,200 check to my parents. To my absolute astonishment, they kept it and cashed it. The cancelled check arrived from the bank, and I marveled at my mother's signature deliberately written on the back of it.

I had no idea that beneath my sincere admission of indebtedness, I harbored the hope that my parents would let me off the hook. I thought I was taking responsibility for my actions when I added my receipts, wrote the check, and announced the staggering amount I owed them. But not until my mom thanked me for the check and tucked it in her purse—and not until my bank balance dropped by twelve hundred bucks in one afternoon—did I become responsible to keep short accounts with others.

Once again, successful kids—contributing kids—take responsibility for their actions, and successful parents hold themselves and their children accountable for doing what's right. Are you tempted to let your kids off the hook before they truly learn responsibility for their actions? Do you cut lessons in responsibility short, before a child's heart is stunned and changed? One way we let kids off the hook is by shifting the blame for their actions (or the consequences of their actions) onto others.

Today, parents blame McDonald's for their children's obesity, Philip Morris for their teenager's nicotine addiction, and "the educational system" for their graduate's illiteracy (if that's not an oxymoron!). We desperately look for scapegoats who can carry the blame for failures that sadden or infuriate us. The trick, though, is determining what part of the load is ours to carry; learning to carry it humbly, graciously, and truthfully; and equipping our kids to carry their load in the same way.

Adults need to reveal to young people that if they step up to an opportunity, admit their wrongdoing, face their lack of investment in a class, or take responsibility for damage they've done, they won't fall apart; they'll grow. Unfortunately, we've watched many of the kids we teach and mentor move toward accepting responsibility for their actions (and the consequences to follow) only to see their parents grab hold of convenient scapegoats to shelter their kids from blame. A daughter skipped school because her friends "tricked her into taking off." A child failed a class because "the textbook was confusing." A son refused to take out his eyebrow ring because he's the victim of "impossible rules and silly consequences." Through such deflections, attention gets diverted from real causes, and kids are "protected" from real change.

As educators in both boarding and day schools, public and private schools, we've also witnessed the torment of teachers who, because of their own misdeeds and failings in their youth, believe they can't hold kids accountable for theirs. Quite often, their fear of hypocrisy overrides a child's need for accountability. For example, a teacher says, "I drank like a fish as a teenager. How can I turn this kid in for drinking when I was just as bad—maybe even worse—myself?" Or "Look at how much this child has already been through! How can I expect anything more from her?"

As parents and mentors, we must uphold justice, offer mercy, and keep walking humbly with God (Micah 3:6) as we hold kids responsible. We need to admit and alter our own irresponsible behavior, admitting as appropriate our own failings to our kids. If nothing else, our mistakes should equip us to communicate with compassion, mercy, and understanding to kids who are being as irresponsible as we once were. But we can't flinch when asked to uphold what's just and right. By introducing kids to fitting consequences, we train them to be wiser than we were and, more important, as wise as God intends them to be.

Barriers and Breakthroughs

What are you doing right when it comes to taking responsibility for your actions and holding your kids accountable for theirs?

In what areas could your kids benefit from greater accountability? (Areas where you've told them what you expect but rarely hold them to those expectations.)

What's your best excuse for not holding your kids accountable for their actions? Why do you let them off the hook?

Reflect on this statement from *Children At Promise:* "Many children will never understand the grace of a true fresh start until they grapple with consequences that build personal responsibility" (p. 103).

One evening, I (Mona) was tempted to wipe the slate clean after a tearful confession about a lie from one of our kids. But the morning after, that child and I walked together to school so the lie could be confessed to our child's teacher as well. As painful as that confession was for our child, the teacher's words of forgiveness and her loving hug sealed the lesson and truly allowed for a fresh start. Are you ever tempted to offer your child a shortcut (instead of a true "fresh start") by not enforcing consequences or requiring full confession?

At-Promise parenting and teaching begins with altering our presuppositions. When it comes to responsibility, we must believe that (1) losing comfort is often required to gain responsibility, (2) blaming others delays growth and shields kids from seeing where *they* need to change, and (3) when we blame kids for our wrongs, we skew the truth and distract them from their own responsibilities. Which of these ideas hits you the hardest or makes the most sense? In what ways?

How good are you at "owning your own stuff"? At admitting your faults to your kids or others? (For example, using destructive anger, avoiding issues, not listening, being critical or negative, lecturing, working too much, lying, disrespecting your spouse.)

How do you respond when your kids excuse their failures by pointing to another cause? Are you relieved that at least it's not their fault? Do you remind them of their ability to act responsibly regardless of the circumstance? Or are you torn?

Do you honestly believe that all kids are responsible for their actions—not necessarily for what happens to them but for their response to what happens? Why or why not?

Jessica's mother, June, greatly values unconditional love and wants her daughter to know she's accepted and forgiven at all times. As a result, she hesitates to enforce consequences that might lead Jessica to question her love. Unfortunately, Jessica now expects her mom to overlook her snarky comments at breakfast, her broken curfews on the weekend, her immodest clothing, and her stack of IOUs. June feels torn. She rejects Jessica's behavior but can't bring herself to discipline her. One day, June realizes that by neglecting discipline, Jessica has missed the point of unconditional love altogether. Her daughter has rarely felt the security of a firm love that confronts her behavior, calls her to a higher standard, and loves her even if she stays angry and rebellious for some time. Jessica must learn that her mom's love survives rejection, rebellion, and disobedience but doesn't overlook it.

Do you see yourself or one of your children in this account? Where? Do you think your kids see unconditional love as one endless act of forgiveness or as an unwavering commitment that's tested and proved through consequences, tough decisions, and natural outcomes?

Striking the Flint

"Judgmental criticism of others is a well-known way of escaping detection in your own crimes and misdemeanors. But God isn't so easily diverted. He sees right through all such smokescreens and holds you to what you've done. . . . Better think this one through from the beginning. God is kind, but he's not soft. In kindness he takes us firmly by the hand and leads us into a radical life change" (Romans 2:3–5, *The Message*).

Cutting to the Chase: Frequently Asked Questions

What specific steps are involved when a child takes responsibility for his or her actions?

Dr. Thomas Lickona, author of *Educating for Character: How Our Schools Can Teach Respect and Responsibility,* identifies five aspects of taking responsibility. Here's our adapted version of his five A's.[1] Kids learn responsibility as we teach them to do the following:

1. *Admit* when they are wrong. Everyone makes mistakes. Assure your kids that they'll make them too.

2. *Apologize.* Better yet, encourage kids to apologize by naming their offense. This is humbling but helps kids own what they've done. Apologizing may involve restitution—for example, returning a stolen item, fixing a broken object, rewriting a plagiarized essay, or paying for lost goods. This is responsible behavior.

3. *Ask* for forgiveness. Encourage kids to seek forgiveness both from those they've wronged and from God. Aim for reconciliation, if possible.

4. *Alter* behavior. Responsible kids respond to consequences with change and growth.

5. *Anticipate* our own apologies for wrong behavior. Offer kids a picture of confession whenever appropriate.

Do I need to hold my kids accountable for every little thing? Won't that drive us buggy?

Yes, it will. It will also be counterproductive. The point of accountability is to help kids get to the point where they *desire* to do what's right and admit what's wrong *based on their sensitivity to the Holy Spirit*—not our nagging. We want kids to tune in to wise voices besides our own. Sometimes natural consequences speak most clearly. For instance, letting a child fail a spelling test when he chooses not to study (rather than studying for him every night while he bucks the process). Sometimes focusing on one or two areas at a time can help as well. It's easier to consistently enforce (and devise) appropriate, logical consequences for a few responsibilities you value most.

Are you saying that kids are never victims? That they are solely responsible for everything that happens to them?

Absolutely not. Sadly, horribly, children are victimized all the time. However, we embitter our kids—and weaken them—when we teach them that the circumstances they face are fully responsible for what they will *become*. That's simply not true, and it short-circuits their quest for a life that's larger than their pain.

Do you have nagging questions about teaching kids responsibility that we haven't answered here? Write them in your Observation Journal and then raise them with your spouse, colleagues, friends, or Breakfast Club the next time you meet.

Assessing Responsibility for One's Own Actions

Worksheet 8.1 gives you an indication your child's willingness to take responsibility for his or her actions. The results should give you a sense of whether taking responsibility is one of your child's strengths or an area that needs work.

Have your child complete the worksheet now. (If your child is eight or younger, you may want to read the questions aloud or complete the assessment on your child's behalf.)

Assessing Responsibility

1. When things go bad for me, it is often someone else's fault.   Yes   No

2. I often do not feel in control of my own life.   Yes   No

3. It seems that life has not been fair to me.   Yes   No

4. When I fail, it is often not my fault.   Yes   No

5. Many things happen to me that are beyond my control.   Yes   No

6. Even if I work hard, people don't notice it.   Yes   No

7. Some teachers give me bad grades because they do not like me.   Yes   No

8. I find it hard to solve problems on my own.   Yes   No

9. If I were somebody else, life would be easier.   Yes   No

10. Sometimes I feel that there is nothing I can do to change myself.   Yes   No

Worksheet 8.1.

Scoring: Simply add up the "No" answers to determine your child's score. Record these results in the At-Promise Profile at the back of the book. A score of 6 or more suggests that your child has a strong sense of responsibility for his or her actions. A score of 3 to 5 suggests an average sense of responsibility, and a score of 0 to 2 suggests a tendency to blame others for what happens to him or her.

Growing Strong Through Relationships

Teaching kids responsibility requires action. Children learn new skills when parents and mentors deliberately instruct them. For starters, we may need to point out specific needs that require a response: a lonely girl in need of a friend, muddy bikes begging for a good rinse, or teeth in need of flossing. After that, we can teach kids how to respond to those needs and to others they notice. By teaching kids skills (how to invite a friend over, how to hook up the water hose, how to wrap floss around the fingers), they gain the "ability to respond." After a task is complete, checking on your children's work and affirming their labor holds them accountable for their actions. It's OK to point out areas that need improvement at that time. Just don't be discouraging or make negative generalizations that kill their motivation to act the next time a need arises.

Observation Guide

For kids, taking responsibility extends beyond simply doing homework and chores. (We're not sure if that's good news or not, but it's true!) Observe how responsible your children are over the next week, using the following categories to guide you:

Personal hygiene (more and more self-regulating by age twelve)

Spiritual well-being (making their hearts open to God and others, praying)

Attending classes and investing in schoolwork

Caring for family members (not just being cared for)

Care and improvement of property (bikes, cars, clothes, furniture, yard)

Responsible and loving care of pets

Admitting personal wrongdoing and accepting the consequences that follow

Keeping promises and fulfilling commitments (including chores)

Following the rules and guidelines of a given community (home, school, activity)

Taking care of friends and friendships through kindness, trust, concern, and generosity

See if your kids are taking responsibility, avoiding it, or oblivious to it in these areas. Record even simple thoughts in your Observation Journal. For example, "John washed his bike and dried it off with a bath towel today. I guess I need to show him where the rags are." Most of the areas of responsibility we've listed continue through life and into lifelong relationships (like marriage), only with greater and greater consequences for irresponsibility. No matter how hard it is to see kids reel under our discipline now, we can take comfort from knowing that accountability and consequences at six or even sixteen sting far less than they do at thirty-six.

A Prayer for Responsibility

What do you want or need God to do for you and your family when it comes to taking responsibility for your actions? What is your prayer for your kids? Write your thoughts below, or pray them as you're most comfortable.

CHAPTER 9

Optimism
Real Tonic for a Toxic World

We won't let those thunderclouds get in our way.

—Paul Ratmeyer, age nine, eyeing approaching storm clouds
minutes before a baseball game with our son, Tyler

An optimist is the human personification of spring.

—Susan J. Bissonette

We who lived in concentration camps can remember the men who walked through the huts comforting others, giving away their last piece of bread. They may have been few in number, but they offer sufficient proof that everything can be taken from a man but one thing: the last of the human freedoms—to choose one's attitude in any given set of circumstances, to choose one's own way.

—Viktor Frankl

Getting Ready

Looking for a more optimistic life with your kids? Begin by reading or revisiting Chapter Eight, "Optimism," in *Children At Promise*. As you do, remember that optimism results from a *faith* perspective, not a *fake* perspective. In this chapter we won't ask you to "put on a happy face" (to mask your confusion or concern about kids), to deny adversity, or to play hide and seek with trouble. Instead, we'll give you a picture of something we call *honest optimism* and help you consider ways that such a gift could transform your relationships with kids.

Connecting

After reading the Optimism chapter, use the following prompts to capture your response.

I agree . . .

I wonder . . .

I hope . . .

Real Life: Where the Journey Begins

I (Mona) grew up with the king of optimism. Not only did my father believe in positive thinking (about everyone and everything), but as Tim writes in *Children At Promise,* he possessed a "contagious" optimism that energized and motivated almost everyone he met. But for some reason, I didn't catch the bug.

As an adolescent, I was like a kid tuning in to foreign programs on a crystal radio set. I searched the airwaves for reasoned voices, voices untinged by what I considered glib optimism, voices tethered to spiritual and intellectual *reality,* voices I could trust. The fear of being "duped" by possibility thinking drove me toward scholarship, critical thinking, and arguments against "blind hope" and easy answers. It was clear to me that suffering existed, things fell apart, and people hurt. Those views didn't make me a pessimist, of course. I simply chose "realism" over unqualified optimism.

But since then, I've had to come to terms with this: the world needs overcoming. My kids have things to overcome. I have things to overcome. And it's faith that overcomes the world (1 John 5:4), not simple realism—and certainly not pessimism. The At-Promise perspective helped me reconcile my need for perspective on both the tragedies and the possibilities of life. It affirms that risk is real, that we will have trouble in this life, and that kids and parents hurt. But it is also utterly optimistic. It teaches us that suffering is not the enemy of hope but the beginning of it and that nothing is too powerful to defeat the promise God has for each person. Out of it, I've found the most honest optimism I've ever known. Optimism that asks me to look squarely at the struggles my kids face today and to see each one as a building block rather than as a wrecking ball of their future promise.

Digging In

Author Adam Khan has it right when he says, "It's an age-old battle. Pessimists think optimists are foolish; optimists think pessimists make themselves unnecessarily miserable."[1] This chapter appeals to both groups and those in between. It asks die-hard optimists to admit that life includes trauma, sadness, and difficulty. It asks die-hard pessimists to admit that defeatism is unproductive and that hope deserves a second chance. And it asks us all to consider the benefits of becoming more optimistic in our care for kids.

Essentially, our pessimism in parenting and mentoring comes down to this: we have trouble believing that trials, struggles, and failures contribute positively to a child's life. So when things go "wrong," we get discouraged. We think that our children's illnesses, disabilities, character and behavior flaws, rebellion, and academic failures attack their chances of living a fulfilled and beautiful life. The result? Defeatism, guilt, melancholy, fear, pessimism about the present and the future—and withdrawal.

As well, too many parents, teachers, and mentors quietly surrender to failure in their relationships with kids because they believe they've already "blown it." Not only did they fail to play Mozart concertos to their baby in the womb, far worse, they were preoccupied, angry, insensitive, or ignorant. They didn't bond with their kids "by the book." Truly, if our failures and inadequacies with children could be listed, we'd hang our heads. But we cannot, we must not, stop there.

Certainly, loving affection, careful instruction and discipline, security, and attentive care are absolutely essential in a child's early years. However, when we believe that a child's opportunity for positive formation expires at three years of age or five (at the latest), we set ourselves up for defeat. Such deadlines do not factor in God's ability to transform messy beginnings, and even messier journeys, into inspired endings. They leave many a parent feeling fatalistic because they've simply made too many mistakes too early in their children's lives, and the damage, they conclude, is likely unredeemable.

But At-Promise parenting and teaching cling to the fact that everything is redeemable. Everything. *Absolutely everything.* Although early parenting mistakes have their consequences and our failure to cuddle, nurture, enjoy, and play with our children does negatively influence their development, surrendering to pessimism because of our mistakes or because our children will "never fulfill our expectations" is more dangerous than anything we may have failed to do right in the past. We can't afford to check out on our kids. Pessimists give up. Optimists stay on course and continue to invest, contribute, believe. Honest optimists can have tears dripping off their chins as they continue to hope. But they continue. Pessimists give in to helplessness and abandon the promise that is just waiting for a second chance—a second look—from a believing parent, teacher, mentor, or grandparent. Abandoning optimism is serious business.

Optimism is a choice we can make at any stage of our parenting, mentoring, or teaching "careers" once we reject the notion that risk is more believable than promise. We can be optimistic about our children's future because we know that even the most difficult and gut-wrenching experiences can and will be used to build them into the contributing adults they were created to be. (Suffering leads to perseverance, which leads to character, which in turn leads to hope.) Our optimism does not come from pretending that adversity does not exist. It comes rather from facing the worst and realizing that it cannot cut us off from God's love, companionship, and care. This fundamental belief gives us very little room for pessimism.

Barriers and Breakthroughs

Perhaps you need a moment to record your response to the thoughts just expressed. Feel free to write a prayer, journal your thoughts, confess your feelings of defeat, or perhaps recommit yourself to believing in a certain child's promise. The space is yours to use as you wish.

Who is the most optimistic person you know? What characteristics reveal that optimism? How does the person's positive outlook affect you?

Is one of your children (students, grandchildren) particularly pessimistic? How does that child's pessimism influence his or her relationships, efforts, and contributions?

When children realize that they can choose their response to adversity and overcome it, they develop a "can do" attitude. Do you think your children understand that optimism can be learned—that optimism is a choice? Or do they react to life as though most circumstances are beyond their control?

Dr. Martin Seligman, America's foremost psychological authority on optimism, asserts that optimism can be learned. He says the change from pessimism to optimism hinges on the way a person views and explains adversity. Those who explain setbacks as permanent, far-reaching, and entirely personal tend to be pessimists. Those who explain setbacks as temporary, limited in effect, and not entirely personal tend to be optimists.[2] We don't believe it's positive to shift responsibility for failures to outside sources, but we also don't believe it's healthy for a child to personalize failure in a helpless way by saying, "I'm dumb," "I'm poor," or "I'm always discriminated against." Such explanations kill motivation because the child seems permanently banned from success based on conditions he or she thinks are beyond personal control.

When something "goes wrong" in your family, how do you explain the situation to yourself, your kids, and others? Do you tend to see setbacks as long-term catastrophes or as short-term growth spurts? How do your kids explain setbacks?

When you look at children in your neighborhood, home, or classroom, are you more likely to see them half full (with promise) or half empty (with shortcomings)? Think of specific children as you answer this question.

As strange as it might sound, do you honestly want to be happy and content about your kids, your family, and yourself (as a parent, educator, mentor), or does optimism make you feel uncomfortable? Do you feel that you might sacrifice reality if you give in to a positive outlook? What reality?

Striking the Flint

"Hope deferred makes the heart sick, but a longing fulfilled is a tree of life" (Proverbs 13:12).

"I consider that our present sufferings are not worth comparing with the glory that will be revealed in us" (Romans 8:18).

"In all my prayers for you, I always pray with joy . . . being confident of this, that he who began a good work in you will carry it on to completion" (Philippians 1:6).

"But hope that is seen is no hope at all. Who hopes for what he already has? But if we hope for what we do not yet have, we wait for it patiently" (Romans 8:24c–25).

Cutting to the Chase: A Frequently Asked Question

In Children At Promise, *you point out that the self-esteem movement has failed to create optimistic children. Are you saying that self-esteem is a bad thing?*

Appropriate self-esteem is essential for kids. The problem is that self-esteem has been hijacked and in many cases turned into a combination of empty flattery and overprotection. Well-meaning parents and teachers are convinced that a failing grade, a lost part in the school play, a rude comment from a friend, or some truthful (though painful) feedback about a piano performance will ruin kids. Why? In part because adults believe that painful experiences prevent kids from succeeding and may be unbearable for them to handle. Also, many adults experienced these assaults as children without any loving interpretation of them from a trusted adult. They want to spare their kids the wounds they know only too well. Optimism then becomes extremely fragile, and parents must constantly guard against any action, word, or experience that might shatter a child's ego. This attitude also leaves children feeling isolated when things go wrong. Everything is about the child, not the community or the greater good.

Children with inappropriate self-esteem feel good for a while until they realize that despite their inflated English grades, they can't write a literary essay; that despite tons of praise about their virtues, they can't deal with constructive criticism; and despite their protected childhoods, they're anxious and hesitant about the future.

From an At-Promise perspective, however, children become increasingly optimistic as they realize that their value is not linked to performance, that they are capable of mastering skills (always and only through overcoming difficulty), and that painful experiences contribute to—rather than detract from—their lives. This kind of optimism gives kids appropriate self-esteem that can be tested by both failure and success but isn't dependent on either one. It encourages and equips kids to maximize their gifts and talents (playing the cello or rebuilding a car engine) by facing the struggles that excellence demands. And it prepares kids to believe that life's difficulties can be allies rather than threats to their fragile assortment of strengths. It offers the kind of self-esteem that can be solidly optimistic in any circumstance.

Assessing Optimism

Worksheet 9.1 gives you an indication of your child's level of optimism. The results should give you a sense of whether optimism is one of your child's strengths or an area that needs to be helped along.

Have your child complete the worksheet now. (If your child is eight or younger, you may want to read the questions aloud or complete the assessment yourself on your child's behalf.)

Scoring: Simply add up the "Yes" answers to determine your child's score. Record these results in the At-Promise Profile at the back of the book. A score of 6 or more suggests that your child has a positive outlook on life. A score of 3 to 5 suggests an average level of optimism, and a score of 0 to 2 suggests a tendency toward pessimism.

Growing Strong Through Relationships

Why is it important to "grow strong through relationships" in the area of optimism? Does it really matter if your kids are a little pessimistic around the edges?

Assessing Optimism

1. I am looking forward to tomorrow.	Yes	No
2. I know that I can be happy even when bad things happen to me.	Yes	No
3. I try to see the good in every situation.	Yes	No
4. I am not afraid of doing hard things.	Yes	No
5. I like my school.	Yes	No
6. I like the saying, "Don't worry, be happy!"	Yes	No
7. People love me and help me get through hard times.	Yes	No
8. I know that God will never leave me.	Yes	No
9. Having a good attitude is very important.	Yes	No
10. I smile and laugh a lot.	Yes	No

Worksheet 9.1.

Martin Seligman did a fascinating study with the Berkeley swim team prior to its exceptional performance at the Seoul Olympics. He first tested the whole team for optimism. Then he gave each team member a setback. In repeated timed heats, the athletes swam a length of the pool and back again. After each heat, the coach reported their times.

As elite athletes, the swimmers knew what their target times should be for each heat. However, as a part of the study, the coach gave each one a slower time than their actual result. He introduced them to a little setback in their daily routine—to a small dose of "planned failure."[3]

The result? In their next heat, the optimists swam *faster* and the nonoptimists swam *slower*. Adam Khan's commentary on this study provides some perspective on the implications for our children: "Imagine the difference in response to setbacks extended over a lifetime of daily hurdles. . . . If every little setback is responded to with fighting spirit, you'll succeed a lot more than if every little setback makes you give up."[4]

We can help kids respond to setbacks so that they are energized rather than defeated by them. You can start now by applying the following tips.

Be there for your kids when times are tough. Nothing lifts us in our darker moments quite like the friendship and companionship of a caring, hopeful person. The very fact that a child is left alone during misfortune can confirm that life stinks and no one cares. Having someone present (not all-wise and all-knowing, just present) confirms the opposite: life can't stink too badly if people still care about me. Notice kids during times of crisis and loss. Talk to them. Put a hand on their shoulder. Offer a few words of hope that feed that child's soul ("I'm here. I wouldn't want to be anywhere else right now" or "You watch. We're going to make it through this together").

Start paying attention to how you and your kids interpret even little setbacks. When one occurs talk or, better yet, write about what you think the setback means. Then consider your interpretation. Have you allowed the event to dampen more of your life than it really needs to? Have you overgeneralized its consequences? Take the time to rethink and rebut your own conclusions (and to help your kids do the same). Just "thinking positive" won't train your mind to undo some of the negative wiring that's been deeply imbedded in your thoughts. Habitual negativity doesn't change without deliberate rethinking and intentional effort to find the truth in your circumstances.

Observation Guide

It's not only film subjects like Forrest Gump who know that a mother's optimism can keep a soul alive. Martin Seligman's research shows that "children's antennae are constantly tuned to the way their parents, particularly their mothers, talk about causes of emotionally loaded events. . . . Mostly they listen closely when you spontaneously explain why things happen—which you do, on average, about once a minute during speech. Your children hang on every word of the explanations you give, particularly when something goes wrong. . . . Young children listen to what their primary caretaker (usually their mother) says about causes, and they tend to make that style their own."[5]

This revelation ought to inspire us to examine exactly what we believe about misfortune. As we'll see more clearly in the next chapter, what we believe influences what we say and do. It also influences whether we and our children will adopt optimistic or pessimistic explanations for life events. Remember, pessimists attempt little, accomplish little, and criticize much. Optimists are healthier, accomplish more, forge stronger (and happier) relationships, and may even live longer. Which prospect would you rather offer *your* children?

In the week ahead, keep your own antennae tuned to the way you and your kids talk about disappointments, losses, hurts, bad news. How do you and your kids naturally explain difficulty or misfortune? Record your thoughts and ideas in your Observation Journal. Also write about changes you think you can make to live more optimistically with your kids. Examine the beliefs behind the words you use, and be open to changing ones that hinder you and your children from going after life (and meeting challenges) with a "can do" attitude.

A Prayer for a Hope-Filled Life

Job's extraordinary trust takes our breath away when he declares, after losing his children and his fortune, "The Lord gave and the Lord has taken away; May the name of the Lord be praised" (Job 1:21). And it catches us again when he says of God, "Though he slay me, yet will I put my hope in him" (Job 13:15). Trust makes optimism possible. It opens us up to God's ownership, workmanship, and training. Without such openness, hope-filled prayer becomes difficult. We ask, and maybe plead, for changed circumstances that will "give us something to be optimistic about," but we don't anticipate God's goodness in our current situation. Do you need to grow in trust and hope? Do you trust God to train you and your kids, or are you discouraged by his shaping and his plans for you? Use the space below to tell God what keeps you from viewing your life, your kids, or your future with optimism. Then, in your own words, reaffirm your trust in God's plans for you, "plans for good and not for evil, to give you a future and a hope" (Jeremiah 29:11).

CHAPTER 10

Motivation from Identity

Claiming Our True ID

In the world to come, I shall not be asked, "Why were you not Moses?" I shall be asked, "Why were you not Zusya?"

—Rabbi Zusya

Before any human being touches us, God "forms us in secret" and "textures us" in the depth of the earth, and before any human being decides about us, God "knit us together in our mother's womb." He loves us with a "first" love, and wants us to be His beloved children.

—Henri J. M. Nouwen

It's not what they call you; it's what you answer to.

—Unknown

Getting Ready

If our identity were easy to understand and accept, far fewer teenagers would trek through Nepal or backpack across Europe to "find themselves" every year. Each summer a new batch of young explorers travels the well-worn paths of "pilgrims" before them, trying to make sense of their place in the world (or at least of their place in Corfu). Having worn those paths ourselves, we certainly cheer them on. However, we also recommend that parents acquaint their kids with an identity that is so secure, so immovable, and so true that a visit to the Dalai Lama will pale in comparison with the truth they've understood about themselves. To help equip you and your kids for this task, read or reread Chapter Nine in *Children At Promise*, "Motivation from Identity," before completing the rest of this chapter.

Connecting

What new insights or revelations did you pick up from reading "the Identity chapter"?

Real Life: Where the Journey Begins

While working at a boarding school in Switzerland, I (Tim) led twenty sophomore students on a cultural trip to France one spring. As we waited for our meal at Planet Hollywood in Paris (I'm ashamed to admit), I scribbled a phone number on the back of my business card. One of my students curiously asked to see the card, and soon all the boys were passing it around. Then, to my surprise, they started reaching into *their own* wallets and adding *their own* business cards into the mix. Credentials were flying.

To be honest with you, I felt pretty good about my business card—until I read theirs. These fifteen-year-old boys held titles that spanned the business world, from marketing directors to sales managers to part-owners of multinational corporations—at least on paper. Grafted into their parents' international businesses, their identities didn't necessarily match their titles (yet). But their business cards sure *looked* impressive.

One card, though, stood out among the others. Written entirely in Arabic, it belonged to a boy named Sultan, the son of a Saudi prince. I asked, "What's this? What does it say?" Sultan explained that the first line was his name. The second line said "son of" and then his father's name. The third line said "son of" and then his grandfather's name, and so on, back seven generations. Other than those seven names, the card was blank. I looked at him and said, "This isn't a business card, Sultan! This says who you *are*. But what do you *do*?" Without hesitating, he looked back at me and answered politely, "Sir, who I am *is* what I do."

Without a doubt, the student schooled the teacher that night—and continues to do so. Years later, I find myself turning this story over in my mind, trying to capture the ways that a person's *being* influences the person's *doing*. I ask myself, does my identity as a child of God dictate my behavior in the same way that Sultan's royalty influenced his actions? If our spiritual identity is the seed of our behavior and ultimately of our destiny, we need to give it some serious thought.

Digging In

Let's review something before we go any further. At-Promise thinkers believe two things about the identity of kids: 100 percent of kids are at risk (they live in a flawed world and possess a flawed nature that cannot please God on its own), and 100 percent of kids are At Promise (they are made in the image of God, with His purposes etched out for their lives from eternity). Children will be motivated properly only if they understand both aspects of their identity: their humanity and their promise in Christ.

The identity kids claim may be false or true, but it motivates their actions nonetheless. A child who sees himself as a loser and a troublemaker tends to lose and make trouble. A child who sees himself as a contributor and a friend tends to contribute and be friendly. The question is, has your child adopted a trustworthy identity? Does it reflect who the child really is before anyone else decides about or defines that child? As written in *Children At Promise,* "identity [from God] is a free gift. Unlike the flighty assessments of people who extend and retract the scepter of fame or popularity or applause or esteem at a whim, God-given identity can't be returned, exchanged, or altered. From birth it extends into every cell of our bodies and into our very souls (Genesis 5:1–2; Psalm 139)" (p. 121).

To help you understand who your kids are, here's a crash course in a child's At-Promise identity.

What Children At Promise Are

• *Made fearfully and wonderfully in the image of God.* As the Scripture references in the quoted passage reveal, God is behind the creation of every child, and each one is designed to be a purposeful reflection of His image. Like God, children possess the capacity for faith, service, love, emotion, change, choice, battle, reflection, invention, creativity, relationship, and communication. This implies that children are chosen by God, not planned by men and women—there's more to their origin and destiny than we think. No child is disposable. Every child, no matter how disabled, debilitated, troubled, or difficult, has something to teach us about the nature of God. Every child is a unique creation with unique gifts and possibilities.

• *Made for eternity.* Ecclesiastes 3:11 puts a child's life story into perspective: "He has made everything beautiful in its time. He has also set eternity in the hearts of men; yet they cannot fathom what God has done from beginning to end." This implies that every issue of a child's identity, character, and behavior doesn't need to be resolved on demand, right now. God makes all things beautiful in His time. We parent for eternity's sake, not just to launch kids into the college years. Then, too, nothing transient or temporary can fully satisfy the longings and needs of a child. The meaning of life, death, and existence ("what God has done from beginning to end") must be explored head on. Every situation has a spiritual dimension.

• *Made of clay.* "Yet, O Lord, you are our Father. We are the clay, you are the potter; we are all the work of your hand" (Isaiah 64:8). "Does the clay say to the potter, 'What are you making?'" (Isaiah 45:9b). This implies that ultimately, we are not the creators or primary shapers of our children; God is. Kids don't reflect us (for our pride); they reflect Him (for His glory). Kids are not divine; they are human. They need God to spark new life in them for their promise in Christ to be realized. We may wonder what God's doing with our kids, but He stands by His workmanship 100 percent. Their weakness is meant to arouse our compassion.

• *Made to overcome.* Humans are made to overcome all obstacles in Christ, not to be defeated by them. Philippians 4:13 was given to me (Tim) by my Grandma Morris as a life verse when I was born on April 13 (4/13), and it has played a significant role in shaping my identity: "I can do everything through him who gives me strength." Importantly, Paul's letter goes on to say in verse 15, "Yet it was good of you to share in my troubles." This implies that we don't let risk factors determine a child's future. As kids find their strength in God, we can expect them to have every resource they need to overcome struggles, addictions, negative attitudes and behaviors, and temptations. Yet it is good for us to share in their troubles, bearing the load together.

• *Made to reveal treasure.* Jesus chose children to reveal His message when He taught on earth. He taught that the greatest in the kingdom are those who humble themselves like children (Matthew 17:4), that it's God's "good pleasure" to reveal things to children that He hides from the wise and scholarly (Matthew 11:25–26), that children must be called to come near, to be blessed and prayed for, because the kingdom belongs to them (Matthew 19:13–15), and that welcoming a child in His name is identical to welcoming Him in the flesh (Mark 9:37). This implies that children are important. They have contributions to make. Children can teach us what Ph.D.'s can't. We miss out when we trade in our relationships with kids to pursue greatness in other places. Children possess greatness without pursuing anything. To be with them is to be with Christ.

• *Made to grow.* Children are made to grow under loving (but imperfect) authority. As much as kids buck the process, both submission to parents and submission to growth are nonnegotiable. This implies that growing pains are part of the childhood package. Kids must learn to follow imperfect people (parents, teachers, coaches, bosses, youth leaders) because no perfect authority (apart from God) exists! Training, correction, instruction, and growth must all factor into a child's life for promise to be fulfilled.

• *Made to choose.* God's first children, Adam and Eve, had the perfect parent, and yet they chose to disregard His teaching. In Hosea, God says of His people, "When Israel was a child, I loved him, and out of Egypt I called my son. But the more I called Israel, the further they went from me." And in Deuteronomy 30:19–20, He says, "I have set before you life and death, blessings and curses. Now choose life, so that you and your children may live and that you may love the Lord your God." This implies that kids can choose right or wrong, life or death, to be wise or foolish, to listen or ignore, to submit or rebel, to blame or take responsibility. We can't choose for them, but we can choose life *ourselves*. We can also hold out the promises that are theirs to inherit if they believe what God says about them.

Barriers and Breakthroughs

Underline the phrases in the section headed "What Children At Promise Are" that catch your attention or motivate you to see kids from a different perspective. Which phrase or statement about a child's identity impresses you most strongly? Why?

What words (positive and negative) do your kids use to describe themselves?

What positive and negative words, descriptions, or labels do you use to describe your kids? Write them down. (Some may be hard to admit or to write down, but naming them can help you understand their impact. Include how you describe your kids to others when the kids are not around, even unspoken words and labels you have used to describe your kids in your own head.)

How have you justified these names or descriptions? What behaviors or attitudes make them seem appropriate?

One mentor asked a child what she would like to be called. The child said, "Why don't you just call me what everyone else does?" "What's that?" the mentor asked.

"Idiot," the girl answered. The mentor went on to call the girl "Roxanne" (her real name), and later she called her "friend."[1] Names are powerful. Have any negative names "stuck" to your kids because of something they've said or done or something that's been done to them ("Klutz," "Crybaby," "Nark," "Klepto")? What are those names?

In *Children At Promise*, I (Tim) tell how my boys picked up a new motivation to treat their sister with respect. I told them, "You are Stuarts. Stuart men don't hit their sisters, they defend them" (p. 131). Statements like this can create a positive family identity for kids. Can you recall any stories about your ancestors or family members that reveal positive traits about your natural or adopted family? Any traits you want to claim for your family starting with your generation? Make some notes, and tell the stories to your kids as a reminder of "who they are" or what kind of people they "belong to."

Sometimes family identity can hinder or even straightjacket a child. I (Mona) taught a girl whose younger brother got into a fistfight on his first day of high school. I asked her what she thought motivated her brother to fight. She shrugged her shoulders and said, "He's a Gordinsky." Essentially, she was saying, "Gordinskys are fighters. What can you expect?" How has your family reputation or identity defined you or your children?

Which aspects of your family identity, if any, have you resisted or rejected? Why?

Apart from God's grace, there's simply no way to FedEx a new identity to kids. It takes time and patience on the part of parents, teachers, and mentors to watch children grow into their true selves. How patient or impatient are you to see your child's promise in full bloom?

The good news is that God specializes in changing names. Better yet, He changes people's names before He changes the people. From impulsive Simon to Peter ("Rock"), from childless Abram to Abraham ("Father of Many Nations"), God predicates every name change on faith, calling us what He empowers us to become. Humans tend to reward others with new names when they deserve them (Top Salesman for 2005, Honor Roll Student, Miss Congeniality). God bestows names on people as a promise of transformation and as an expression of mercy. What identities or names do you wish your children could trade in? What new names would you love your children to be called?

Not everyone likes God's merciful approach (giving great names to great risks). But we need to get over that. We're all great risks! God has good names, good identities, for everyone He creates. He wants us first and foremost to be known as *His child* and to take on *His family likeness.* The truth is, every kind of identity based on changeable criteria (looks, family heritage, behavior, interests, desires, status) is unstable. The only way to entirely break free from negative or temporary identities is to become a new creation—to understand and grab hold of a new and unshakable identity in Christ. ("If anyone is in Christ, he is a new creation; the old has gone, the new has come!"—2 Corinthians 5:17.) In the words of a powerful worship song, God says, "I will change your name. You will no longer be called wounded, outcast, lonely, or afraid. I will change your name. Your new name shall be confidence, joyfulness, overcoming one, faithfulness, friend of God, one who seeks my face."[2] When we take on our identity in Christ, our motivation changes; we are free to be what our Maker intended without being fueled to prove ourselves through fleeting accomplishments or family expectations. Have you let God adopt you into His family so that these names can become yours? Have your children?

Striking the Flint

On our way back from a family trip to the Grand Canyon, we overheard a sidewalk conversation in Flagstaff, Arizona, between a teenage girl and a middle-aged woman. The girl insisted that she had a driver's license, but the woman adamantly pointed out that the girl wasn't even sixteen, the legal driving age. How could she have a license? Finally, the girl revealed her winning hand: "Well, I never said it wasn't fake, but I do have a driver's license."

The New Testament talks about Christ humbling Himself and "being found in appearance as a man." Though He was God Himself (not just an image bearer but the very image itself), He was often mistaken for an ordinary man in His life and death. His great glory was humbled in human circumstances (Philippians 2). And so people wanted Christ to admit that He was packing fake ID when He walked the earth. They accused Him of parading as God when they knew He was *really* just "Joseph's son," an ordinary guy from Nazareth.

Likewise, children fearfully and wonderfully made in the image of God may be found in the *appearance* of a druggie, an angry child, a "privileged" child, a juvenile delinquent, a self-sufficient child, a dropout, a promiscuous teen, a rebellious child, or even a "lost" child. These disguises tempt us to think that "all we see is all we get." But this is not so. God's image is there, intentionally camouflaged in a child's flaws or weakness because human weakness is God's chosen showcase for His glory. Scripture tips us off about this:

> If you only look at us, you might well miss the brightness. We carry this precious Message (treasure) around in the unadorned clay pots of our ordinary lives. That's to prevent anyone from confusing God's incomparable power with us. As it is, there's not much chance of that. You know for yourselves that we're not much to look at. We've been surrounded and battered by troubles, but we're not demoralized; we're not sure what to do, but we know that God knows what to do; . . . we've been thrown down, but we haven't broken [2 Corinthians 4:7–9, *The Message*].

Beware of assuming that a kid who is "not much to look at" is a child without promise. Beware of wanting your child to be the treasure instead of being a vessel for the treasure (God Himself). No doubt, kids will try to make sense of themselves apart from truth. They will pass themselves off as all kinds of things that don't necessarily reveal their true identity. Our job is to help them surrender their fake ID so they can claim the most accurate picture of who they are and were created to become. If we simply concentrate on the visible, on the mug shot they've carefully copied, cut, and laminated, we will be misled. If we look further and pray further, we will await the revelation of Christ's design and workmanship in them as they *claim* their true identity.

Whose fake ID have you fallen for lately?

Cutting to the Chase: A Frequently Asked Question

How should a child's identity cause us to view bullying and physical or other kinds of abuse?

Our role is to respect, defend, and love children, not to abuse them in any way. As bold as it might be to say this, it's likely that some people reading this book have taken advantage of children without being discovered. In the hidden corners of their parenting, teaching, and child care, they silently break kids' hearts and cover the evidence. Maybe they've thought that because the At-Promise philosophy makes room for adversity in kids' lives, the adversity they've inflicted on others can be overlooked. Underneath, though, they are waiting for someone to say, "No! You *must* stop hurting children. You will grieve the Holy Spirit, the spirits of children, and your own spirit as long as you continue." That *is* what we're saying here. If you're hurting kids, you must stop. Frank Peretti, a survivor of childhood bullying, puts it this way in his book *No More Victims:* "I believe that every human being has value, meaning, and dignity. Why? Because we matter to Almighty God! Moreover, not only is it wrong for me to devalue another person, to belittle, to bully, or to abuse another person, but I must do what I can to defend those who cannot defend themselves from such abuse."[3]

Assessing Identity

Worksheet 10.1 gives you an indication of your child's self-concept. The results should let you know whether your child has a positive sense of identity or if this is an area that is still being formed.

Assessing Identity

1. I know that I am a very special person.	Yes	No
2. My family is important to me.	Yes	No
3. I feel good about who I am.	Yes	No
4. I know that I am a child of God.	Yes	No
5. I have talents and skills that I love to use.	Yes	No
6. I believe that I was created for a special purpose.	Yes	No
7. I know that I can overcome difficult times.	Yes	No
8. I know that I am loved even when I do something wrong.	Yes	No
9. I like being a part of a team.	Yes	No
10. I know that God did not make a mistake when He made me.	Yes	No

Worksheet 10.1.

Have your child complete the worksheet now. (If your child is eight or younger, you may want to read the questions aloud or complete the survey yourself on your child's behalf.)

Scoring: Simply add up the "Yes" answers to determine your child's score. Record these results in the At-Promise Profile at the back of the book. A score of 6 or more suggests that your child has strong sense of his or her own identity. A score of 3 to 5 suggests a positive sense of belonging, and a score of 0 to 2 suggests a weaker concept of his or her identity.

Growing Strong
Through Relationships

The most important thing we can do to help children develop a positive identity is to remember that there's more to their lives than we see at any moment and to hold on to our "magic eye" image of them over time. Pointing out our children's strengths and the noble family attributes they mirror, encouraging them to identify with healthy role models, and creating a current family identity that kids can embrace are all helpful.

However, kids need to confirm their identity independently, and the process can be messy. I (Mona) remember challenging my conservative father with endless Marxist and leftist ideologies at the supper table when I was in college. On many occasions it likely appeared that I was ready to sign on as a card-carrying Communist. But I pushed against him to establish the firmness of my starting point, to see if my roots would hold or not. In reality, I was memorizing my father's well-founded rebuttals and taking comfort in the fact that he could handle the debate.

Kids will push, challenge, explore, and test the firmness of many roots on their path to establishing a solid identity. Many of those roots must cave in on them, and we need to let them cave (their "ultimate job" might end, their sports scholarship get cut, their relationships crumble, their mentors disappoint them). Just like us, our children will *always* be tempted to define themselves by transitory things (what they have, do, and know or what they don't have, don't do, and don't know). Our job is to pray, instruct, and support them until they find themselves "rooted and grounded" in Christ above all else. Then their motivation for doing, knowing, having, and being will take off in fantastic directions.

Observation Guide

Think and write about just one question in the coming week: What do I really value when it comes to my child's identity? Think about the comments you make, the values you hold, and the desires you have for your child's future. What's behind those expectations? Does your influence (your words, actions, and expressed expectations) make your child more or less secure about who God made him or her to be? This would be a great question to consider among friends or with your Breakfast Club. (Keep in mind that when children fulfill their God-given identity, their lives will likely be filled with accomplishments, contributions, and recognition. Don't be afraid of valuing contribution. All kids are made to contribute, too!)

A Prayer of Affirmation

The following prayer affirms a child's God-given identity and confesses our need to see children as their Creator does. Use it to pray for your children, students, grandchildren, or other kids you love. Insert each child's name in the blanks to personalize the prayer for individual children.

Creator God, I want to affirm the identity you designed for _____. I want to exchange my feeble sketch of _____'s promise for the magnificent picture you hold of him (her) in your hand. Before any human being decided about _____, you loved him (her). Before labels, before strengths and weaknesses, before judgments about looks and brains and personality, you loved this child with an everlasting love, and you still do.

I affirm that you've placed eternity in _____'s heart and made him (her) endlessly long for you in ways that nothing else can satisfy. Don't let _____ rest until he (she) finds that rest in you. Help me see beyond flesh and blood and the here and now. Keep me from rushing this child's growth. I affirm that you'll make everything in _____'s life beautiful in your time.

Lord, I admit that _____ is made of clay. I accept his (her) humanity and weakness and trust you to shape him (her) into a vessel that brings you honor. Forgive me for questioning your skill and your workmanship as the Potter at times. Forgive me for being more exasperated than compassionate with _____'s weaknesses. He (She) belongs in your good hands for good reason.

Sometimes I think _____ is made for endless struggle or endless ease. But you have made him (her) for endless overcoming. Thank you for designing this child to draw on your power for every struggle so that he (she) can face life head-on. Give us your power to go through trouble together and come out stronger on the other side.

_____ can teach me. When I welcome him (her), I welcome you in the flesh and learn about your kingdom without pomp and ceremony. When I spend time with _____, I spend time with the greatest in your kingdom. How wrong I've been to think that greatness lies everywhere else but in the presence of children like _____.

Many times I've felt that _____ is stuck—too stubborn or too fragile for change in certain areas. But I see that you've made _____ for growth. As imperfect as my influence is, you want him (her) to grow under the wing of my love and authority—and under yours. Help me instruct, correct, discipline, and forgive _____ with a humble heart.

Finally, Lord, _____ has choices to make, and I can't make them for him (her). O God, teach him (her) first to desire—and then to choose—life over death, submission over rebellion, good over evil, wisdom over foolishness, Christ over self. His (Her) freedom scares me to death, but I give _____ to you. Your kingdom come. Your will be done in his (her) life as it is in Heaven. Amen.

CHAPTER 11

Integrity
A Mirror of the Soul

Today's go-getter parents and today's educational institutions work frantically to cultivate neural synapses, to foster good study skills, to promote musical talents. We fly our children around the world so that they can experience different cultures. We spend huge amounts of money on safety equipment and sports coaching. But when it comes to character and virtue, the most mysterious area of all, suddenly the laissez-faire ethic rules: You're on your own, Jack and Jill; go figure out what is true and just for yourselves.

—David Brooks

Integrity is the principle which gives bridges, buildings, companies, families and people their completeness and strength.

—Millard "Mac" MacAdam

There can be no friendship without confidence, and no confidence without integrity.

—Samuel Johnson

Getting Ready

This chapter takes us beyond the sorry lack of ethics we find in any number of public figures—politicians, performing artists, and business moguls alike. It takes us where our watercooler and playground gabfests rarely reach—into the heart of our *own* integrity and our children's integrity. For as much as we yearn to be led by people we can trust (and find ourselves appalled when that trust is betrayed), our personal "balance sheets" could use an audit now and then as well. To prepare yourself for this stretch of the journey, it would be good to read or reread Chapter Ten, "Integrity," in *Children At Promise*.

Connecting

If you could pull any three quotes, stories, or ideas from the Integrity chapter to share with others, what would they be and why? Write them down here and share them with your Breakfast Club members the next time you meet.

Real Life: Where the Journey Begins

Our three kids went through an insufferable phase where they insisted on starting arguments, asking for snacks, or making raucous noise every time Tim or I (Mona) answered the phone. This habit really pushed my buttons. I'd try cutting off their antics with exaggerated charade moves—my hand slicing across my throat while I gave them the sternest looks I could muster. Almost inevitably, though, I'd end up excusing myself from the phone.

"Just a minute," I'd say to my friend. Placing my hand over the receiver, I'd then *blast* my kids for their insolence. "Can't you see I'm talking on the phone? Can't you be quiet for just a few minutes? You know the rules! Now leave me alone and let me finish talking!" After pelting my kids with rejection, I'd return to the phone. "Sorry about that. Now, where were we?"

Several months into this phase (I told you it was insufferable), Tim called me from work. The kids revved up their distractions and, predictably, got the best of their mom. I excused myself, covered the receiver, and snapped at the kids. When I returned to the phone, Tim asked, "Did you cover the receiver just now?" "Yes," I said without thinking. Tim was silent and then broke the horrifying news: "Mona, I just heard every word you said."

My brain went numb. I tried to review all the comments I had made to my kids while trusting I was under the protection of my carefully cupped hand. It's probably a mercy that my memory failed me. I was mortified. More than that, I was sobered because I thought I could separate my private dishonor from my public self. I had spoken to my kids in a tone I never would have used if I'd known that other people were listening.

Is there an aspect of your life that you would be mortified to discover had been completely visible or audible to others while you assumed it was under cover? God's mercy helps us admit these things on our way to becoming whole people and whole parents.

Digging In

Our integrity gives children the stability and strength they crave. It confronts our inconsistencies; it drives our hidden faults into the open; it makes us practice what we preach (and acknowledge it when we don't); it compels us to do what's right; it straightens every crooked part of us that might injure others. Over time, it can even stabilize kids who've been horribly wounded by the betrayal and deceit of others. In a word, integrity makes us trustworthy. By clinging to values that are more sacred than any immediate comfort, convenience, advantage, or appearance, we offer kids a solid life over merely a good-looking one.

But in spite of these benefits, integrity is a hot potato. It's great when other people have it, but the longer we hold it ourselves, the more we fear it will burn us. After all, integrity requires a commitment to honesty and consistency in every aspect of our lives—but who can attain it? And how can we promote it without becoming either hypocrites for eventually compromising our own standards or fools for trying to uphold standards that no one takes seriously anyway? Knowing our temptations and weaknesses, the pursuit of integrity can seem like a setup for failure. Rather than break our standards and let kids down in the process, it might be better not to profess any at all, we think.

In addition to these insecurities, we've become increasingly and dangerously cynical about the role that values, ethics, and morality should play in our lives. Many adults and kids today question whether moral values are even acceptable anymore, much less worthy of upholding. As Dr. Robert Shaw points out in his book *The Epidemic,* "We live in a society that has in great measure drifted into a moral relativism in which there are very few things that are categorically wrong to do. . . . We're on the far side of the spiritual parabola, where it isn't politically correct to consider moral training as central to child-rearing."[1]

But without clear values and morals, integrity has no starting point: it has nothing against which to measure itself. A child's cheating can be rationalized from every angle these days—as a chemical imbalance, a result of stress, a function of competition, an understandable temptation—to the point where it seems insensitive for an adult to simply call it "immoral." The distinct edges of right and wrong have been blurred almost beyond recognition, and now parents are floundering as they attempt to pass on values to their children while being morally skittish and apologetic themselves.

So what do we do? How do we respond to the failure of integrity in our society, in ourselves, and in our children? Well, first of all, we recognize that there's a correlation between the rejection of values and ethics in society and the various traits that now mark what Dr. Shaw would call "the nasty generation"[2]: a lack of empathy for others; blatant and shameless cheating, lying, bullying, and stealing; violent crimes against peers; disrespect and aggression toward authority; and a moral helplessness that keeps kids from finding clarity and peace in their relationships. We simply can't abdicate our responsibility to teach our kids values through relationships and still expect to produce decent, loving, compassionate, and responsible children.

Second, we need to deliberately define or reclaim the specific values that will shape our lives, and we need to start living those values *every day.* This is no casual task. We don't just scribble our values on a napkin while sipping a latte at Starbucks. But that might be a fine place to start. In fact, why don't you grab a cup of coffee or find a quiet place and then think through the following questions about your values and the role of integrity in your home. To get the maximum benefit from this exercise, you'll then want to have some serious talks about these questions and answers with your spouse, a friend who knows you well, your Breakfast Club members—perhaps all of them.

Barriers and Breakthroughs

Can you identify the top four or five core values that guide you and your children? If so, write them down now. If not, start brainstorming about the values that matter most to you. Use your Observation Journal for more space, if needed.

On what do you base your values? Are your values tied to some code or spiritual standard, or are they flexible and personal? How have you decided that they are essential?

What steps are you taking right now to teach or to reinforce your most cherished values to your children or grandchildren? What steps *could* you take to do that?

Most parents and teachers respond to so many disciplinary issues in a day that they can lose sight of their basic, nonnegotiable expectations. What rules and expectations do you have for children in your home or classroom? List them now. Could your children or students clearly list and explain your rules, if asked to?

How do you enforce your expectations through active discipline (training) and close relationships (support)? What happens when a child doesn't meet your expectations?

Our children "live in a country that has lost, in its frenetic seeking after happiness and success, the language of sin and character-building through combat with sin. Evil is seen as something that can be cured with better education, or therapy, or Prozac. Instead of virtue we talk about accomplishment."[3] While education, therapy, and Prozac have their place, does the "language of sin" have a place in your worldview as well? Does a child's lack of integrity indicate a need to "combat sin" in some area, or can everything be chalked up to weaknesses, limitations, or circumstances?

Integrity involves both upholding the standards we value and admitting our failure to uphold them. It's a mandate for transparency. The "garage door" story on pages 135 and 136 of *Children At Promise* has captivated many readers and has given them a powerful metaphor for understanding how integrity and transparency coexist. What's your response to that story? What does it teach you about integrity in your own life?

What activities, relationships, habits, or pursuits are preventing you from living a life of integrity right now? What do you need to change, abandon, or confess to straighten things out? How willing are you to do those things to gain integrity?

Striking the Flint

"Search me, O God, and know my heart; test me and know my anxious thoughts. See if there is any offensive way in me, and lead me in the way everlasting" (Psalm 139:23–24).

In an age of flexible and convenient morality, the idea that God should search our motives and behavior according to His standards is quite foreign. But when we renew our desire to be obedient to Scripture and allow our consciences to once again be sensitive, responsive, and alert to God's spirit, integrity has a chance to grow in us from the inside out.

You see, real integrity requires a kind of wholeness and completeness that can only be worked into us by the Spirit of God: a wholeness of heart, mind, and body called holiness. Again and again, as we open ourselves to the Word and the Spirit, God will bring our hidden and festering actions into the light for healing. He'll show us where we missed the mark (conviction) and ask us to admit our wrong (confession). He'll ask us to turn away from our sins (repentance) and mend our relationships with others (reconciliation). And He'll give us new fervor and strength to live in agreement with His values (renewal). This is the cycle we'll repeat for a lifetime. It's the cycle of authentic growth that leads to integrity. We can make endless attempts to be men and women of integrity under our own power, but not until we allow God to search us and try us—to see if there's any compromising way in us—will we live with real integrity.

"For the word of God is living and active. Sharper than any double-edged sword, it penetrates even to dividing soul and spirit, joints and marrow; it judges the thoughts and attitudes of the heart. Nothing in all creation is hidden from God's sight" (Hebrews 4:12–13).

"Now, O Lord our God, . . . we have sinned, we have done wrong. . . . We do not make requests of you because we are righteous, but because of your great mercy. O Lord, listen! O Lord, forgive!" (Daniel 9:15–19).

Cutting to the Chase: A Frequently Asked Question

Is integrity an "all or nothing" character trait, or can a person develop integrity by failing and making mistakes?

If pursuing integrity means avoiding any compromise, you might as well tear out this chapter and use it to light your bonfire, because we're all toast. Parents who believe that every compromise or failure they make places an irreparable dent in their integrity can be tempted to either hide their wrongs or to abandon integrity's pursuit. That's not only sad but also unnecessary. A blameless and upright life is a life that is lived without disguises, not a life that's lived without wrongs. In fact, both struggles and strengths can build our integrity if we expose them truthfully, transparently, and humbly. If there's anything I (Mona) love about the At-Promise perspective, it's that it's chock full of truth and the highest ideals for every child and caring adult, but it is equally crammed with grace for all the failures and mistakes we will make. And so the At-Promise focus on succeeding through moral and social contribution rather than acquisition allows us to take the honest path even when honesty might block our promotion, scar our reputation, or prevent us from achieving immediate status. We need not cover our tracks, deny our faults, cheat to get ahead, or pretend to be something we're not because ultimately those approaches don't lead to true success anyway. Instead, we succeed by doing what is right—even acknowledging and taking responsibility for our failures as they occur.

Assessing Integrity

Worksheet 11.1 gives you an indication of your child's sense of right and wrong. The results should let you know whether your child has strong convictions about integrity or if this is an area of weakness.

Have your child complete the worksheet now. (If your child is eight or younger, you may want to read the questions aloud or complete the assessment yourself on your child's behalf.)

Scoring: Simply add up the "Yes" answers to determine your child's score. Record these results in the At-Promise Profile at the back of the book. A score of 6 or more suggests that your child has a strong sense of integrity. A score of 3 to 5 suggests an understanding of the difference between right and wrong, and a score of 0 to 2 suggests a weakness in the area of integrity.

Growing Strong Through Relationships

We train kids to have integrity most effectively by having integrity ourselves. When we lose a house deal because we're honest about the leaky basement, when we return the extra 29 cents that a cashier mistakenly added to our change, when we admit to

Assessing Integrity

1.	I tell my parents when I get into trouble at school or at a friend's house.	Yes	No
2.	I know the difference between right and wrong.	Yes	No
3.	I do what is right even when it is hard.	Yes	No
4.	Even if it hurts, I keep my promise.	Yes	No
5.	I admit when I do something wrong.	Yes	No
6.	I obey the rules at school.	Yes	No
7.	I ask permission before using other people's things.	Yes	No
8.	I feel better when I tell the truth.	Yes	No
9.	When I hurt someone's feelings, I apologize on my own.	Yes	No
10.	I feel bad when I do something wrong.	Yes	No

Worksheet 11.1.

our kids that we disciplined them in anger and apologize for it, we show our children how integrity looks and feels. At times our integrity will shock them ("Why didn't you just keep the change? It's only 29 cents!"). At others times it will spell incredible relief ("It feels good to know that when you're wrong, you'll admit it").

If we don't pursue integrity ourselves, we will likely lack the humility to respond graciously to our kids when they do. When they admit they're having sex instead of secretly going on the pill, when our son confesses that he broke the team rules and gets booted from the regional tournament as a result, or when our daughter pulls out a broken vase (our favorite) from behind the couch, our own admissions and confessions will remind us that a gracious and merciful response is a difficult but beautiful thing.

The trust we want our children to place in us and their freedom to confide in us will grow as they see integrity and trustworthiness in our own lives. Integrity starts with our example.

Observation Guide

For the week ahead, here's a three-part observation assignment. Once again, take notes in your Observation Journal as you consider these integrity issues.

1. Notice how you confront your kids about gaps in their integrity (for instance, when they lie, cheat at a game, ditch a friend, or refuse to acknowledge their wrongdoing). Are you lenient, severe, balanced, or oblivious? Why? What fears or concerns motivate your response? (Maybe you're lenient because you want to spare your kids the shame and embarrassment of "getting caught," or maybe you ignore their offenses because you're afraid your kids will go ballistic or go underground with their activities if confronted.)

2. What do you and your kids do when you sin (when you violate God's values)? Do you tend to admit it, ignore it ("Sin? What sin?"), seek reconciliation, turn in a new direction, try harder next time, hope no one notices, or cover your tracks? What's your most common response, and why do you respond that way?

3. Keep your eyes open for an "integrity dilemma" in your home or at work. Write it down and share it with your Breakfast Club members or a close friend. For

example, if your daughter accidentally took a candy bar from a store, you might ask your group whether, in the same situation, they would be more likely to go with her to return it, return it for her, put it in their pocket and tell her to pay more attention next time, or ask her to return it on her own. You could consider the pros and cons of these different approaches and discuss what took place in real life. Learn from each other!

A Prayer for Cleansing

Sometimes our prayers lack integrity. They don't come from the bottom of our hearts. For example, we may be ashamed to admit, even to ourselves, that we are hiding something from God—anger toward a child or spouse, lingering frustration over the role we play in the world, resentment toward a neighbor, or guilt about unkind words we've spoken. But God is looking for worshipers who will "worship Him in spirit and in truth" (John 4:24)—who will be themselves in His presence.

As you prepare to pray honestly about the state of your heart and any hidden issues you may need to confess to God, take comfort in remembering that He sees not only our wrongs but also our circumstances, our strengths, and our progress. He says, "I know your deeds, your hard work and perseverance. . . . I know your afflictions and your poverty. . . . I know where you live—and where Satan has his throne. Yet you remain true to my name. . . . I know your deeds, your love and faith, your service and perseverance, and that you are now doing more than you did at first. . . . I know that you have little strength, yet you have kept your word and have not denied my name" (Revelation 2:2, 9, 13, 19; 3:8). Most of these affirmations from Christ to the churches in the book of Revelation are followed by a *yet*. He goes on to pinpoint their wrongs, but not without first affirming and speaking all that is right and good in them. Take heart from this, and in the space below, confess to God whatever is hidden or wrong in your life. He loves you extravagantly, He knows you intimately, and His mercies never come to an end.

CHAPTER 12

Service

It Takes Two Brooms to Change the World

I don't know what your destiny will be, but one thing I do know: the only ones among you who will be really happy are those who have sought and found how to serve.

—Albert Schweitzer

Give every part of your heart and your time to God and let God tell you what to do, where to go, when and how to respond.

—Henri J. M. Nouwen

The secret of living is giving.

—Jim Janz

Getting Ready

If you've wondered where love is found in At-Promise character, this is the place. Service clears a spot in our self-absorbed lives for compassion, humility, love, and concern to take root. Through it, God empties us of our hoarded ambitions for ourselves and our children and fills us with a hunger for true success. Go ahead and read or reread Chapter Eleven, "Service," in *Children At Promise,* and then we'll consider how service makes room for God's great gifts to grow in our lives and relationships with kids.

Connecting

Did this chapter strike a chord with you (or a nerve perhaps)? What examples, ideas, or facts about service caught your attention? What questions or concerns did the chapter raise? Write these down so you can discuss them later with your Breakfast Club, your spouse, or a close friend.

Real Life: Where the Journey Begins

Kurt Hertzen had to *feel* his way out of trouble because he certainly couldn't *see* his way out. Diagnosed with juvenile diabetes at the age of three, hit by a drunk driver at nineteen (resulting in a severely damaged retina and the end to a competitive baseball career), and left with impaired vision from both circumstances, Kurt slid into an alcoholic and destructive stretch that lasted five years.

Near the end of that slide, he was home with a newborn daughter but without a job or a visible future. He was barely making it on his annual $12,000 from Social Security and his wife's $7-an-hour salary. At that point, Kurt decided to get advice from a friend and counselor. "At the time, I was twenty-five years old, now disabled, feeling pretty useless," Hertzen remembered. "[My friend] told me to go out and do something for somebody else. I thought he was crazy. I thought somebody should be doing something for me."

Fortunately for Kurt, he respected his friend enough to follow his advice. He started volunteering as a greeter and guide at Havasu Regional Medical Center in Lake Havasu City, Arizona. "That's right . . . I was a blind tour guide," Kurt jokes. He confesses that he took the job with a "self-pitying attitude" but that he emerged with some surprising gifts in tow: gratitude, of all things, and a "brighter outlook for the future." Service opened his mind to new possibilities for his future.

Now Kurt is thirty-one. In the intervening years, he not only went through forty eye surgeries to prevent total blindness but also propelled a fledgling vending machine business into a financial success, grossing over $400,000 last year. In fact, Kurt was named Arizona's Vendor of the Year by the Business Enterprise Program for the Blind three years in a row.

Listen to what Kurt now says about the significance of learning to serve: "I found out for myself that until I got out there and started to put one foot in front of the other, and doing and giving selflessly, I wasn't receiving the gifts of life. I never use my disability as an excuse for anything, because it's not."[1]

Digging In

I (Tim) like Kurt's story because it reminds me that everyone can serve and can benefit from serving, too. As the principal of a largely Native American and low-income high school, I want my students to understand that they have much to give away to others. Although our school and community are often the recipients of service projects and mission trips, I want our gifted, unique, and beautiful kids to realize that their community and school are not only marked on the map as *destinations* for service trips but as *departure points* for their own service as well. In fact, every home should be a departure point for service.

Still, it's hard to tell a guy like Kurt Hertzen to pull himself off a sagging couch and think of someone else's needs, isn't it? Most of us look at a young man like him— disabled, poor, drinking himself silly—and say, "That guy needs help." We're not so quick to say, "That guy needs to serve humanity." After all, don't certain unfortunate kids have enough problems of their own? Is it really fair or *kind* to expect them to contribute while they're suffering? (And beyond that, is it fair to ask children to serve? Shouldn't we be serving them?) Yet it was service that ended Kurt's self-pity even though his painful circumstances continued for some time. And service is God's remedy for selfishness in all of us, no matter how strung out or pulled together our lives may appear to be.

So why do a child's success and character growth depend on serving others? First of all, because success and service are inseparable twins. Keep in mind that At-Promise thinkers measure success by a child's contribution (service to others) rather than his or her acquisition (of education, wealth, status, and so on). It's only in giving that children become great. Scripture gives this thinking the thumbs up. Jesus taught, "If you want to be great in God's kingdom, learn to be the servant of all" (Matthew 20:26). Jesus is saying that in the only kingdom that counts—His kingdom—the great ones serve others. If we are raising our children to please the only king who matters, we simply *must* train kids to serve. But is this the kind of success we really want for our kids and ourselves, the self-emptying kind? The humble kind?

Just think of all the time, energy, and cold, hard cash we spend trying to lift our kids to greatness without expecting them to serve! Think of all the ways we make our children our cause without necessarily training them to serve the great causes of justice and mercy in this world![2] And then let's ask, Am I training my kids to be *truly great*, or am I encouraging them to pursue a *counterfeit greatness* (in which service is only an option or an afterthought but not a requirement)? Do my kids know how to serve skillfully, generously, and willingly? These are hot questions, we know. We hope it comforts you to hear that they fall like firebrands on all of us. We all have so much to learn, model, and teach our kids about service.

Before thinking through our own barriers and breakthroughs about serving others, here's an overview of how service benefits kids:

- Service puts their needs in perspective: "I thought my life was rough, but you should see how this lady on Grover Street lives."

- It moves them from "a sense of entitlement to one of gratitude" (*Children At Promise*, p. 146): "I was fuming because my parents wouldn't buy me a Mustang for graduation, and then I met these kids on our trip to Haiti who can't even go to school."

- It tells them they're not alone in their pain: "When I helped at the hospital fundraiser, I met kids who've had even more surgeries than I have. I couldn't believe it."

- It helps them look for and listen for the needs of others: "I had no idea old people could be so sad and lonely until I visited my grandma at the retirement home. Next time, I want to bring them some flowers."

- It makes them dependent on God's strength: "I was so nervous to bring Mom's lasagna to our new neighbor that I even prayed as I walked over there. She was happy I came."

- It helps them see what they have to give: "I thought the poem I wrote for Mrs. Stansbury was pretty stupid, but she tacked it on her wall and even cried when she read it."

- It humbles them: "Jake is a mess since his parents split up, and I don't know how to help him. All I can do is listen."

Each of these benefits fulfills a need in a child's life: a need for perspective, gratitude, community, sensitivity and compassion, dependence on God, the stewardship of unique gifts, and humility. By serving others, kids pick up the character traits of greatness without knowing it, and that's a powerful type of learning.

Barriers and Breakthroughs

Would you say that serving others comes easily for you, or is service a more deliberate and difficult choice for you? What holds you back from serving others or inspires you to serve others?

Before reading *Children At Promise*, what role did you see service playing in a child's success? In your own success? How has your perspective changed?

Can you trust that serving others will make your kids successful, or do you fear that truly successful people focus on acquiring position, titles, degrees, and promotions while the servants are left to fulfill inferior tasks?

"Watching our children serve, lecturing them about serving, or financing their service is not enough. To teach service, we must sweep alongside our kids" (*Children At Promise*, p. 149). We teach a child to sweep by bringing two brooms: one for the child and one for ourselves. In what ways have you been "sweeping alongside your kids"? What chores or tasks do you do together? What tasks *could* you do together?

Do your kids routinely sit back, expecting others to serve them (entertain them, finance them, clean up after them, organize and take care of them), or do they jump in to help others? How do you feel about the contribution each one is making to the *moral* and *social* fabric of your home?

Walter Wangerin laments, "My second son, whose back ripples with quick strength on the basketball court, is suddenly crippled by the mere mention of the lawn mower."[3] How do your kids respond when you ask them to help with household chores or to go out of their way to serve others?

Does the phrase "I might as well do it myself" sound familiar? Let's face it, it's easier (and tidier) to bake cookies ourselves than to bake a batch with kids who love cookie dough but who lack baking skills. The same goes for mowing the lawn, washing the dishes, and weeding the flowerbeds. How tempted are you to do chores or tasks for kids because it's just simpler and more efficient that way? What's the hardest part about allowing or teaching your kids (or grandkids) to serve?

Do you think that you're raising your kids to be *skilled* and *willing* servants? Why or why not? What would need to change for them to become more skilled, more willing, or both?

A child becomes truly successful when the gifts he or she possesses are used to bless and care for others. Think about an activity or skill in which your child excels. It might be gymnastics or pottery, lacrosse or writing, baking or chess. Take a couple of minutes to brainstorm how service to others could be a part of your child's success in that area. (Maybe it's offering to sweep the lacrosse box after practice or to cut up oranges for a game. Maybe it's making pottery vases to hold wildflowers for sick friends or teaching a younger child to play chess.) How could your child serve with his or her gifts?

Most of us have "special kids" in our lives—kids we mentor, neighbor kids who hang out at our house, foster kids, grandkids, nieces and nephews. What tasks could you ask these kids to do when they're around? What jobs could you do together? What skills could you teach them?

Striking the Flint

"We know love by this, that He laid down His life for us—and we ought to lay down our lives for one another. How does God's love abide in anyone who has the world's goods and sees a brother or sister in need and yet refuses to help? Little children, let us love, not in word or speech, but in truth and action. And by this we will know that we are from the truth and will reassure our hearts before Him whenever our hearts condemn us; for God is greater than our hearts, and He knows everything" (1 John 3:16–20).

Write a response to this passage.

Cutting to the Chase:
Frequently Asked Questions

Is it OK for us to ask our grandkids to help with household chores and projects even though we only see them once in a while? Our time with them is so short that we want every minute to be happy. (And quite truthfully, we don't want the grandkids to think we're ogres.)

Grandparents, mentors, or others who may spend only short bursts of time with children can be tempted to leave service out of the picture. Time is short, life is beautiful, and won't it sour things if I ask the grandkids to pitch in? Perhaps. Some kids will get bent out of shape when you ask them to help. But from our experience, some of our children's best memories with their grandparents include watering flowers on the terrace, feeding the dog (using *all* their "dog French" at Tim's parents' house in France!), steering Grandpa's boat through the San Juans, tearing down the remains of an old greenhouse with cousins (at Grandma's command), picking berries, and stacking winter wood.

These kinds of activities (with margin for lots of fun and play, too) graft kids into family, home, and heritage and communicate how capable they are of contributing. Just make sure that your expectations are realistic and that you're game for some spills and mistakes. Through service, your grandkids will gain an inheritance of skills, relationship, and memories by working together with you. Don't hesitate to offer them that!

I'm confused. How do I lay my life down for my kids and still expect them to serve? I feel guilty asking my kids to help around the house because I think I should be taking care of all their needs. How do I make sense of this?

This question reveals a significant conflict for parents. On one hand, how do I serve my kids sacrificially without crippling their own ability to serve? On the other, if I'm a true servant, should I expect my kids to serve too, or should I just "do everything" for them? And here's a thornier question yet: If I devote myself to my children's welfare, will my kids learn by my example to serve others, or will they become bloated, demanding and lazy, always expecting others to cater to their every whim?

It's interesting that Jesus laid down His life for us but also taught us to lay down *our* lives, to take up *our* cross, and to *follow* Him. He washed His disciples' feet but turned around immediately and taught them to wash each other's feet according to His example. A teacher's goal is to replicate his life, example, and teachings in his students. Obviously, we don't want to pass on a "servanthood" to our kids that's tainted by guilt, anger, or frustration, which can happen when we bear the load alone. Martyrdom and servanthood are not the same thing. Our homes should become places where we serve in the example of Christ, as devoted and willing servants, but also as disciplers of our children. Equipping and expecting them to serve is, in itself, a great act of service.

Keep in mind that just when you think your kids have gotten the hang of service, they may hit their teen years and not want to do a darn thing around the house. Take heart. Their lessons learned about serving still remain intact, even though it may take a year of rooming with a slob at college (or four years of rooming with a bunch of slobs) before they circle back and begin to serve at home. Be patient and keep asking them to lend a hand.

Assessing Service

Worksheet 12.1 gives you an indication of your child's disposition toward serving others. The results should let you know whether your child is in the habit of serving others or if service is an area in which your child needs to be strengthened.

Have your child complete the worksheet now. (If your child is eight or younger, you may want to read the questions aloud or complete the assessment yourself on your child's behalf.)

Assessing Service

1.	I enjoy helping others.	Yes	No
2.	I have many things to be thankful for.	Yes	No
3.	I believe that it is important to help others when they need it.	Yes	No
4.	Many people have needs I could meet.	Yes	No
5.	I do not complain when my parents ask me to do chores around the house.	Yes	No
6.	When I grow up, I want to have a job that helps people.	Yes	No
7.	Being with people who need my help makes me realize how good my life is.	Yes	No
8.	When I need help from people, I am willing to ask for it.	Yes	No
9.	I happily say "you're welcome" when someone thanks me.	Yes	No
10.	I like helping people before they ask me for help.	Yes	No

Worksheet 12.1.

Scoring: Simply add up the "Yes" answers to determine your child's score. Record these results in the At-Promise Profile at the back of the book. A score of 6 or more suggests that your child demonstrates a disposition toward serving others. A score of 3 to 5 suggests a growing understanding for the importance of service, and a score of 0 to 2 suggests a need to reinforce the importance of service.

Growing Strong Through Relationships

Along with consistent and loving discipline and academic rigor, service is one of the few areas that allow us to structure a little "controlled adversity" in our children's lives. Although we can't plan other forms of adversity, we can handpick their service assignments and offer them the support they need to get the job done.

However, we need to introduce service to kids in doses they can swallow and digest. You'll alienate your unsuspecting kids if you suddenly draw up the "Master Calendar of Service to Home and Country" and act like a drill sergeant as you order them into action. Better to start with a couple of well-chosen assignments that you will take the time to schedule, teach, model, and inspect. Don't assume that your child knows how to clean the toilet *properly* or to organize his room *according to your standards.* Walk through it with him. Do it together a couple of times. Keep supplies in a place where your child can find them. And be positive! It's one thing for the *job* to be miserable, but don't make your kids gag on service because *you're* miserable, too. Your positive instruction, correction, and inspection can help kids acquire a good appetite for service.

Observation Guide

While writing this chapter, our powers of observation have become focused on service in our own home. Soon yours will be focused on service within your own four walls. May God help us all. As a couple, we've come to the conclusion that service is hard for us to teach our kids because we don't model it very well, we don't like it very much, and we don't really want to be successful after all.

Actually, based on our experience, we'd like you to do two things this week. First, observe all the ways that your kids serve spontaneously. Be on the lookout for their "random acts of service" at home and elsewhere. Jot these down in your Observation Journal, along with any insights they inspire. Second, list all the ways you require your kids to serve at home, and describe how your kids respond to those. Which child is convinced that service is a form of adversity? Who thrives on serving others? Who disappears when the dishes need washing? Through this exercise you'll discover how willing your kids are to serve. You'll also see if their service tends to be more scheduled ("The chore chart says it's your turn to clean the bathroom") or random ("Wow, you cleaned your room! Good for you!"). While you're at it, keep your eyes open for new ways that you can serve your kids, teach them to serve, or work alongside them. Record these discoveries as well.

A Prayer for Serving Others

Recently, when facing my lack of stamina in serving others, I (Mona) read a reassuring confession from Mother Teresa. She said, "Without prayer I could not work for even half an hour."[4] Of all people, you'd think Mother Teresa could work forever by drawing on inner stores of love and compassion. But no. It's not possible for any of us to serve well without praying often.

And sometimes praying is our best service to others. As John Milton reminds us, "They also serve who only stand and wait."[5] Our physical service to our kids has its limits. Through trials and distance we learn over time that our greatest acts of service for our kids are often fulfilled on our knees. All our worry, activity, and exhausting service can't accomplish more for them than a moment of prayer in which we offer them again to their Maker. Have you been making space in your prayers to offer your children's needs to God—and your needs regarding them? Use the space below to seek God's strength for serving others and to serve your kids by offering heartfelt prayers for them.

CHAPTER 13

Engaged Play

The Great Healer

We worship our work, we work at our play, and we play at our worship.

—Gordon Dahl

Getting Ready

What better way to end our journey through this workbook than to spend some time thinking about play! Hopefully, by this point on the trail you've been able to discard some fears and gather new hopes for your children At Promise. This chapter helps us throw off the remaining restraints that hinder us from laughing with, engaging, and celebrating kids through play. Before you tackle it, though, make sure you read or reread Chapter Twelve, "Engaged Play," in *Children At Promise.*

Connecting

How did you respond to the "Engaged Play" chapter? What did it stir up in you? How did it make you feel? Use the following prompts to capture some of your reactions.

I felt . . .

I remembered . . .

I wished . . .

I wondered . . .

Real Life: Where the Journey Begins

Summer break is the ultimate *tabula rasa* for parents and kids: a blank slate to be filled, you'd think, with endless days of barefooted play, hunts for horned toads and blue-tailed lizards, bike rides down Suicide Hill, water fights, and moonlit games of capture the flag. Why is it, then, that within days of their release from the classroom, many kids (including ours) are bored silly and whining about having "nothing to do"? And how is a parent to respond? Especially when that parent still has a book deadline to meet by the end of June? (What were we thinking?)

When I (Mona) felt my patience unraveling, I reconciled the need for both work and play in our family's life by paying a visit to my neighbor Mary Ippel. My trip across the street was actually a pilgrimage to her family fridge. Rumor had it that the Ippels' fridge contained a map to summer sanity and a game plan for structured but independent play. It was a treasure map I needed to see with my own eyes! More than that, I had observed the rhythm of play and service, love and friendship that surrounds the Ippel home and knew that regardless of how the Ippels organized their time in the summer, they understood engaged play.

Taped to the Ippels' fridge were seven nearly identical charts (one for each of their five kids and two visiting cousins). The charts listed activities that each child must complete and check off each day before any TV can be watched or video games can be played. (Page 143 shows such an activity chart, tailored for use with up to three children and ready for you to photocopy.)

At the end of each week, kids whose charts are completely checked off go on an outing with Mom and Dad for ice cream or snow cones. At the end of the summer, an excursion is planned so that the whole family can celebrate.

Here's what we like about this approach to structuring vacation activity with kids:

- By starting each day actively, kids are less likely to mold themselves into the couch later in the day. They learn to find opportunities for play and service.

- Until this chart is completed each day, kids always have "something to do."

- It leaves room for choice and flexibility while providing structure.

- It is useful for a wide range of ages. Currently the Ippels use it (with slight modifications to account for age) with kids ranging from seven years old to college age. Everyone participates every day.

- It incorporates a variety of At-Promise values like service ("Ask for a job," "Do something nice for someone"), engaged play ("Play a game with someone"), and responsibility for actions ("Pick up your things," "Make your bed").

An added bonus for working parents is that each day, whether your kids are with a sitter or old enough to be on their own, basic chores are completed, the house is picked up, and your kids use a good portion of their morning in constructive but fun activities. Instead of nagging about unmade beds and wasted TV time the minute you walk in the door, you can reserve your energy for engaged play with your own children!

Digging In

Children At Promise defines engaged play as a kind of play that connects us with kids and that replenishes our strength and perspective. Such play is uncomplicated. It doesn't require game pieces, rented ponies, or a master's degree in outdoor education. We don't have to hoard glue and scissors to make it work. In fact, just two simple qualities distinguish engaged play from other types of play.

First of all, it's *relational*. Engaged play demands our attention and our interest in kids regardless of the activity we're sharing. This kind of meaningful interaction is not satisfied with bowling in separate lanes or dusting the coffee table between turns at Monopoly. That would be *parallel* play, not *engaged* play. To be engaged, we must

Daily Activity	Child:					Child:					Child:				
	M	T	W	Th	F	M	T	W	Th	F	M	T	W	Th	F
Read for 30 minutes															
Practice or play an instrument for 15 minutes															
Do one nice thing for someone															
Exercise for 30 minutes															
Go through the house and pick up your things															
Make your bed															
Walk the dog or draw or write in a journal															
Ask for a job															
Play a game or board game with someone															
Play a computer learning game for 15 minutes															

focus on being with, knowing, enjoying, and affirming children while we play. The activity and its outcome are secondary in our minds to the deeper, positive connection we're creating with a child through it.

Second, it's *re-creative*. It refreshes and restores the family and contributes to our spiritual, emotional, and physical health. Engaged play punctuates our lives with episodes of laughter, abandon, playfulness, and creativity that offset our encounters with adversity and struggle. In that sense, it changes up the pace, adding a Sabbath rest to the laborious rhythm of our lives. This does not mean that we only play on Sunday but rather that we stop our incessant planning, achieving, and performing long enough to realize again that we're children in the hands of God: our lives and our success depend on His goodness, not on our frantic efforts. In other words, our play shouldn't be a continuation of our work. It shouldn't always be competitive, goal-oriented, and driven. It's OK to relax a bit, celebrate, and "dawdle," knowing that far from slowing down the unfolding of our promise or our children's promise by doing so, we actually hasten its fulfillment.

In spite of this knowledge, some of us would rather work overtime than return home to yet another game of "go fish" with the kids. We are haunted by regret over not playing more often with once eager but now distracted children, but we are also torn by our own exhaustion, ambitions, and financial pressures, not to mention the vacuuming, the laundry, and the dirty window we only notice when we sit down to play chess with our son. How do we play with our kids and still get everything done? How do we let kids play when the pressure is on to overschedule them to success? If we pull back the throttle on our kids' more structured activities, won't we be sorry?

The noted journalist David Brooks wrote a stunning article for the *Atlantic Monthly* in 2001 called "The Organization Kid." He spent four months interviewing students and professors at Princeton University, taking the pulse of a new generation of college students—their moral life, their academic life, and their social life. Despite all the credentials, accomplishments, and intellectual feats of these elite students, he noted that the ingredient repeatedly and sadly lacking in their lives was "passion."[1] Since birth, their thirty-something parents had rotated them from "one adult-structured activity to another honed to near-perfection." In the process they had learned performance. They had learned to ace every instructor's expectations, to build a résumé, to gather an arsenal of imposing skills. But they didn't know who they were or what passions were worth working toward, singing about, or fighting for. They were a part of a "vast network" that Brooks calls the "Achievatron."[2]

In the *Wild at Heart Field Manual,* John Eldredge refers to the story of how he became an author and a counselor. His journey began with these words: "Don't ask yourself what the world needs. Ask yourself what makes you come alive, and go do that, because what the world needs is people who have come alive."[3] Some kids have been so channeled and so driven to accomplish from infancy that although they appear successful (and by many standards *are* successful), they have never discovered what makes them come alive. Play can do that for kids. It can give them the freedom to discover what delights them instead of what drives them. It's a gift we can't afford to schedule out of their lives.

Barriers and Breakthroughs

In *Children At Promise,* Cheryl tells the magical story of her summer with the Siemens family in Washington. We love how she explains her entrance into their family: "In a ten-minute drive across town, I went from being the big sister in a serious, chaotic, single-parent home to being the baby in a playful, peaceful family with two parents who loved each other and loved to laugh" (p. 153). Was there a time in your life when you were immersed in a playful, loving environment? What was it like? What did it do for you?

What are your best memories of play as a child? Do any of them include your parents, grandparents, or other adults?

What are your best memories of playing with your own children or grandchildren? What made those times particularly rich?

Would you describe your immediate family as playful or serious? Relaxed or driven? In what ways?

We'd be kidding ourselves to pretend that play with children is a natural delight for every parent. Many of us can't leave the vacuuming, the dishes, or other responsibilities to play a single board game with our kids, or if we do play with them, we check our e-mail or balance our checkbook on the side. What is your biggest barrier when it comes to playing with children—yours or other people's? What prevents you from investing fully in play with them or from wanting to play in the first place?

Certain families rarely play together without tensions and conflicts erupting. "More often than not, when these families try to play, family members will end up isolated from one another (through an argument, misunderstanding, or mistrust), and they will either control or be controlled by each other. Knowing that once again they have failed to have fun together, they may lose hope in their family, if they haven't already" (*Children At Promise*, p. 156). Does this scenario sound familiar to you? Does play disintegrate into squabbles and disappointment in your home? What happens? What do you wish would happen when you play together?

The tendency to focus on rules, winning, technique, or performance can overshadow relationship building in play. While there is certainly time for learning, competition, and winning in gamesmanship, it's important that every episode of play not be dominated by the need to get ahead and stay ahead. How competitive are you and your family members? Do you think that competition forges or strains relationships in your home?

Dream a little. What is your ideal picture of playing with your kids or grand-kids? What would you like to do together, and what would it feel like to be doing that?

Think about the At-Promise kids you teach or know. Could any of them bene-fit from an adventure or an outing with your family? Who? What could you do together, and how could you focus on those children when you're together?

Striking the Flint

"To everything there is a season, and a time for every matter under heaven;. a time to weep, and a time to laugh; a time to mourn, and a time to dance" (Ecclesiastes 3:3b–4).

Though the early stages of a child's life seem like endless work at times, and young parents tire of hearing repeated admonitions to savor the moment (because "they grow up so fast, you know"), inside we know it's true. We know it's not right or wise to rush our children.

Walter Wangerin possesses this wisdom and so instructs us:

Let the children laugh and be glad. O my dear, they haven't long before the world assaults them. Allow them genuine laughter now. . . . Soon enough they'll meet faces unreasonably enraged. Soon enough they'll be accused of things they did not do. Soon enough they will suffer guilt at the hands of powerful people who can't accept their own guilt and who must dump it, therefore, on the weak. In that day the children must be strengthened by self-confidence so they can resist the criticism of fools. But self-confidence begins in the experience of childhood. . . . The laughter that is so easy in childhood must echo its encouragement for a long, long time. A lifetime.[4]

Cutting to the Chase: A Frequently Asked Question

You have no idea how chaotic our home is. I can't even imagine getting to the place where we could set our stress and tensions aside in order to have fun. How can I offer my kids time to play when nothing about our life is playful at all?

This is an honest admission. Many families, even if their lives don't look chaotic from the outside, are locked in a survival mode that leaves little room for play. Recall from *Children At Promise* (p. 129) that Cheryl Bostrom's and Amy Kane's mothers were in this position and allowed their daughters to experience carefree adventures and outings in the company of other families. It's OK to keep your eyes open for At-Promise adults and families you and your kids admire and to arrange blocks of time for your children to spend with them. Also, if group dynamics are not encouraging in your family, look for moments to be good-humored or to joke with a single child rather than expecting the whole family to join in an activity together. In the meantime, look for ways to destress your life. Get in the habit of releasing your struggles in prayer. And get rid of any joyless obligations or unnecessary commitments that prevent you from being available, alive, spontaneous, and lighthearted with your own kids.

Assessing Engaged Play

Worksheet 13.1 gives you an indication of your child's involvement and enjoyment in engaged play. The results should let you know whether your child is engaged in healthy play or if this is an area that requires growth and greater interest.

Have your child complete the worksheet now. (If your child is eight or younger, you may want to read the questions aloud or complete the assessment yourself on your child's behalf.)

Assessing Engaged Play

1. My parents often do fun things with me.   Yes   No

2. I enjoy playing games with adults.   Yes   No

3. I feel happy when I play.   Yes   No

4. I have many friends who are adults.   Yes   No

5. I like to learn new games.   Yes   No

6. I can enjoy playing a game even when I lose.   Yes   No

7. Games are more fun when my parents play with me.   Yes   No

8. I like making up games with my friends.   Yes   No

9. I would rather play than watch TV.   Yes   No

10. I like to have fun in a group rather than playing alone.   Yes   No

Worksheet 13.1.

Scoring: Simply add up the "Yes" answers to determine your child's score. Record these results in the At-Promise Profile at the back of the book. A score of 6 or more suggests that your child is open to developing relationships through play. A score of 3 to 5 suggests an average disposition toward relational play, and a score of 0 to 2 suggests a need for increased engaged play in his or her life.

Growing Strong Through Relationships

Obviously, kids need to learn to play on their own. We are not their sole playmates, nor should we be. But if a child feels cut off from us—always shooed away to play with someone else—our connection with that child as a caring adult can be damaged. Kids will wonder whether we really enjoy them or just want to be with them when we're not preoccupied with more important things. On the other hand, sometimes a child's desire to play with us can be endless. No matter how much time we spend playing ball, answering knock-knock jokes, riding bikes, or making paper airplanes with him, his tank remains on empty.

Here's a helpful strategy for building playtime into your life, whether you're struggling to spend any time playing at all or feel like you're spending too much time playing with your kids:

1. Determine how much time you think you can happily and sanely play with your children each day (maybe it's fifteen minutes, maybe it's an hour or two). Even fifteen minutes a day will give your child an hour and forty-five minutes of undivided, stress-free play time with you a week. Is that more than you're giving him or her right now?

2. Schedule that time into your day. Commit to it. Anticipate it. Let kids know it's coming. You may want to divide it up into a couple of blocks of time in the morning and afternoon or in the evening after work. (Kids can play more willingly on their own knowing that you'll be joining them at a certain time.)

3. Be "all there" when playtime comes. Turn off your cell phone. Put your papers and letters aside. Play where you can't see the dishes or your computer. Focus on your child.

4. Recognize that if you love closure in one activity before beginning another, letting go of the housework in order to play will drive you nuts. If that describes you, you'll just have to force yourself to leave an uncleared kitchen table to play ball with your kids before the sun sets.

Observation Guide

Try scheduling some time to play or to be playful with your kids this week, and then observe how it affects you, your relationship, and each child you spent time with. How hard or easy was it for you to make room for play? How did things go? What were the positives and negatives of your time together?

If you're in the habit of sending your kids or grandkids outside, down to the basement, or into their bedrooms to play, take some time to observe them in action this week. Sit on the front steps with a glass of iced tea and take it all in. What do they play? How do they play? Whom do they play with, and what are their interactions like? What do you notice about your child's interests, ability to share, creativity, strengths, and weaknesses?

Finally, observe the tone of your home and the kind of play you engage in this week. Do people spontaneously initiate play together, or does it have to be "organized"? Is play "parallel" or "engaged"? In other words, do you focus on each other positively when you play, or do you focus on the activity, the game, or the competition while remaining in separate worlds?

A Prayer for a Playful Spirit

O God, play is a gift that we unwrap and enjoy far too seldom with our children. Like worship, it's your remedy for our stress and busyness. It's meant to take our eyes off ourselves and to replenish us with joy. Forgive us for wasting so many moments—when kids pulled on our hands and begged us to play. For not taking a day's rest to celebrate your good creation in our very own kids. Lord, forgive us for using play only to compete with others, conquering even our own children selfishly, impatiently, and unnecessarily. Forgive us for being together in play but not connecting, loving, or noticing each other. Forgive us for feeling so responsible for our work and our homes that we forget we are also your children, made to play and to discover how straight you steer the world even when we take our hands off the wheel.

Help us offer our children space and time to discover the passion in their promise—to know what it is they love to do and to "feel your pleasure" in it as their only reward. For all the difficult jobs ahead and for all the times when work is far from play, do this for us: teach us to play like only your children can. And in the process, give our children joyful memories of play that can be "held in reserve as fuel for hope" when life and love are hard. Amen.

Some Closing Thoughts

At the beginning of this workbook, we set out to explore not only the depths of At-Promise thinking but also our own deeply held beliefs about how children grow best. We set out to deliberately notice the children in our care and to equip ourselves to support them through thick and thin. We began with assumptions to test, fears to confess, strengths to recognize, hopes to protect, and risks to face. And though we've traveled far, our journey is not yet over.

From this point on, each new child and each new trial we meet will give us opportunities to look for promise and to respond in hope. Each day will offer us a chance to contribute positively by doing what is right and by serving others. As we move into that future, we have this confidence: "He who began a good work in [us and in our children] will carry it on to completion until the day of Christ Jesus" (Philippians 1:6). The struggles ahead might tempt us to believe that God's good work is merely a fantasy and that our children's completion is unlikely. Such thoughts naturally assault us as we cross the chasm from struggle to character and hope. They attack our perseverance. But they don't need to rob us of our confidence because God's purposes, intentions, and promises are certain. "Every word of God is flawless; He is a shield to those who take refuge in Him" (Proverbs 30:5).

Although many people may not understand the necessity of trials to your children's success and to yours, find a few close friends who do, who believe that "all things work together for good to those who love God and are called according to His purpose" (Romans 8:28). Gather around you some companions who believe in God's power to uphold and straighten your life when you need to believe it most and who affirm the promise in your children even as they struggle and fall.

Yes, we encourage you to grow strong through relationships with others. To form that Breakfast Club—even if you've already completed this workbook alone. To share your insights and questions with others. To help each other not only survive but surrender to the hope in the adversity you face with your children in the days ahead. For optimism to triumph in our lives and for faith to overcome our doubts, we need to travel together.

Raising Children At Promise isn't about turning our families into trophies for our comfort and pride but about letting God do His work in us so that His purpose and our promise can be fulfilled. It's about accepting our humanity. Allowing our mistakes to land face up instead of face down. Letting ourselves *grow.* Jumping boldly into relationships. Feeling the edges of our promise expand as we trust God to redeem everything, the good, the bad, and the devastating. And it's about continuing to hope for children: to hope that adversity will strengthen instead of harm them and that love will soften instead of threaten them. As we press on, the Comforter, the Holy Spirit, will be our constant companion who will sustain and encourage us until God makes all things beautiful in His time. Until promise finally overcomes pain. And until the image of God appears flawlessly in all children.

We leave you with a prayer for the journey. Pray it often, and travel in peace.

Be still, my soul: the Lord is on thy side.
Bear patiently the cross of grief or pain.
Leave to thy God to order and provide;
In every change, He faithful will remain.
Be still, my soul: thy best, thy heavenly Friend
Through thorny ways leads to a joyful end.

Be still, my soul: thy God doth undertake
To guide the future, as He has the past.
Thy hope, thy confidence let nothing shake;
All now mysterious shall be bright at last.
Be still, my soul: the waves and winds still know
His voice Who ruled them while He dwelt below.

Be still, my soul: when dearest friends depart,
And all is darkened in the vale of tears,

Then shalt thou better know His love, His heart,
Who comes to soothe thy sorrow and thy fears.
Be still, my soul: thy Jesus can repay
From His own fullness all He takes away.

Be still, my soul: the hour is hastening on
When we shall be forever with the Lord.
When disappointment, grief and fear are gone,
Sorrow forgot, love's purest joys restored.
Be still, my soul: when change and tears are past
All safe and blessèd we shall meet at last.[1]

At-Promise Profile

Use the following charts to record your children's scores on the nine character assessments found in this workbook. Use one chart for each child. (Make photocopies if you need more than the four charts presented here.) Each completed chart will give you a visual picture of that child's current strengths and weaknesses in each area. In keeping with the At-Promise perspective, scores are meant to reveal a starting point for growth, not a fixed score or "label" for a child. In areas where a child's scores are particularly weak, be sure to read the "Growing Strong Through Relationships" section in the corresponding chapter to discover relational ways to help your kids grow stronger.

At-Promise Profile for:	Score	Adversity	Relationships	Perseverance	Responsibility	Optimism	Motivation by Identity	Integrity	Service	Engaged Play
	High (6–10)									
	Medium (3–5)									
_____	Low (0–2)									

At-Promise Profile for:	Score	Adversity	Relationships	Perseverance	Responsibility	Optimism	Motivation by Identity	Integrity	Service	Engaged Play
	High (6–10)									
	Medium (3–5)									
_____	Low (0–2)									

At-Promise Profile for:	Score	Adversity	Relationships	Perseverance	Responsibility	Optimism	Motivation by Identity	Integrity	Service	Engaged Play
	High (6–10)									
	Medium (3–5)									
_____	Low (0–2)									

At-Promise Profile for:	Score	Adversity	Relationships	Perseverance	Responsibility	Optimism	Motivation by Identity	Integrity	Service	Engaged Play
	High (6–10)									
	Medium (3–5)									
_____	Low (0–2)									

Notes

Chapter One: A New Look At Promise

1. T. Proscio, "Jabberwocky Junkies: Why We're Hooked on Buzzwords—and Why We Need to Kick the Habit," *Grantsmanship Center Magazine,* Fall 2002, http://www.tgci.com/magazine/02fall/jabber1.asp.

Chapter Three: The Trailhead

1. B. Curtis and J. Eldredge, *The Sacred Romance: Drawing Closer to the Heart of God* (Nashville, Tenn.: Nelson, 1997).

2. Ibid., p. 47.

3. J. G. Adams, *What Do You Do When Fear Overcomes You?* (Phillipsburg, N.J.: P&R Publishing, 1975), n.p.

4. T. K. Merton, *Thoughts in Solitude* (Boston: Shambhala, 1993), p. 89.

Chapter Five: Adversity

1. C. S. Lewis, *The Problem of Pain* (New York: Simon & Schuster, 1996; originally published 1940).

2. Keith Bulthuis, Bethany Christian Reformed Church, Gallup, N.Mex., Mar. 7, 2004.

3. J. C. McMillen and R. F. Fisher, "Table 1: Perceived Benefit Scale Items and Original Item Numbers, by Subscale (Modified)," *Social Work Research,* 1998, *22,* 178. Copyright © 1998, National Association of Social Workers, Inc., Social Work Research. Used by permission.

4. J. C. McMillen, S. Zuravin, and G. B. Rideout, "Perceptions of Benefit from Child Sexual Abuse," *Journal of Consulting and Clinical Psychology,* 1995, *63,* 1037–1043.

5. Adapted, with permission, from a prayer by Keith Bulthuis, Bethany Christian Reformed Church, Gallup, N.Mex., Mar. 7, 2004.

Chapter Six: Trusting Relationships with At-Promise Kids

1. H. Dayton, "The Amazing Impact of Life Investment," *Money Matters, Crown Financial Ministries,* Sept. 2003, p. 8.

2. T. S. Stuart and C. G. Bostrom, *Children At Promise: 9 Principles to Help Kids Thrive in an At-Risk World* (San Francisco: Jossey-Bass, 2003), pp. 75–76.

3. E. H. Peterson, *Where Your Treasure Is: Psalms That Summon You from Self to Community* (Grand Rapids, Mich.: Eerdmans, 1999), pp. 171, 172.

4. Survey items are adapted from *Search Institute Profiles of Student Life: Attitudes and Behaviors,* © 1996, Search Institute, Minneapolis, Minn. Used by permission.

5. P. Scales, "Reducing Risks and Building Developmental Assets: Essential Actions for Promoting Adolescents' Health," *Journal of School Health,* 1999, *69*(3), 113–120.

Part Three: Building PROMISE Character

1. Wisdom Quotes, "Woodrow Wilson," http://wisdom1.jjnet.com/cgi-bin/mt/mt-search.cgi?Include Blogs=4&search=Woodrow+Wilson, Apr. 23, 2003.

Chapter Seven: Perseverance

1. E. H. Peterson, *A Long Obedience in the Same Direction: Discipleship in an Instant Society* (Downers Grove, Ill.: InterVarsity Press, 1980).

Chapter Eight: Responsibility for Our Actions

1. Adapted from a *Family in Focus* radio broadcast featuring Dr. Thomas Lickona, 2004.

Chapter Nine: Optimism

1. A. Khan, *Self-Help Stuff That Works* (Bellevue, Wash.: YouMeWorks, 1999), p. 9.

2. M.E.P. Seligman, *Learned Optimism: How to Change Your Mind and Your Life* (New York: Free Press, 1998).

3. E. Sonnenberg, "Optimism Interview," http://www.youmeworks.com/optimisminterview.html, Mar. 2000.

4. Ibid.

5. Seligman, *Learned Optimism,* p. 128.

Chapter Ten: Motivation from Identity

1. B. Ghezzi, "Calling a Child by Name," *Christianity Today,* Aug. 2003, p. 48.

2. D. J. Butler, "I Will Change Your Name," © 1987 Mercy Publishing. Reprinted with permission.

3 F. Peretti, *No More Victims: An Underdog Who Came Out on Top Challenges You to Put a Stop to Bullying in Your School* (Nashville, Tenn.: W Publishing Group, 2001), p. 39.

Chapter Eleven: Integrity

1. R. Shaw with S. Wood, *The Epidemic: The Rot of American Culture, Absentee and Permissive Parenting, and the Resultant Plague of Joyless, Selfish Children* (New York: Regan Books, 2003), p. 134.

2. Ibid., p. 135.

3. D. Brooks, "The Organization Kid," *Atlantic Monthly,* Apr. 2001, pp. 40–54.

Chapter Twelve: Service

1. S. Dunham, "Disabled Man Accentuates Positive," *Gallup* (N.Mex.) *Independent,* Dec. 10, 2003, p. 11.

2. J. Piper, "A Call for Coronary Christians," http://www.desiringgod.org/Online_Library/Online Articles/FreshWords/2002/012302.htm, Jan. 24, 2002.

3. W. Wangerin Jr., *Little Lamb, Who Made Thee? A Book About Children and Parents* (Grand Rapids, Mich.: Zondervan, 1993), p. 144.

4. Mother Teresa, *Meditations from a Simple Path* (New York: Ballantine Books, 1996), p. 7.

5. J. Milton, "Sonnet XV (On His Blindness)," 1652.

Chapter Thirteen: Engaged Play

1. Brooks, "Organization Kid."

2. M. D. Smith, "Engineered for Success: David Brooks Discusses His *Atlantic Monthly* Article About Today's University Generation," *Response,* Spring 2004, p. 22.

3. J. Eldredge, *Wild at Heart Field Manual: A Personal Guide to Discover the Secret of Your Masculine Soul* (Nashville, Tenn.: Nelson, 2002), p. 250.

4. Wangerin, *Little Lamb,* pp. 19–20.

Some Closing Thoughts

1. "Be Still, My Soul," K. von Schlegel (lyrics, 1752), J. L. Borthwick (trans., 1855), J. Sibelius (music, 1899).

The Authors

Timothy S. Stuart, Ed.D., is the high school principal at Rehoboth Christian School in New Mexico. He is a member of North Carolina's High Plains Saponny Indian Tribe and a Gates Millennium Scholar. Tim was nominated for the Excellence in Teacher Preparation Award by Washington State University in 2001 and has worked with kids as a secondary teacher, coach, and administrator on three continents. The founder and president of At Promise, Inc., Tim speaks widely on the At-Promise paradigm. He and his wife, Mona, have been married for eleven years and have three children. Tim can be reached at tstuart@atpromise.com.

Mona M. Stuart has taught English and mentored junior and senior high school students in both North America and Europe. She also served as a boarding school dorm mom to hundreds of high school girls and as a college counselor before becoming a student of her own three children. Mona speaks at conferences and retreats and is a professional grant writer for nonprofits serving At-Promise youth. Mona can be reached at mstuart@msn.com.

Children At Promise:
9 Principles to Help Kids
Thrive in an At Risk World

Dr. Timothy Stuart, Ed.D.
Cheryl Bostrom, M.A.
Paper
ISBN: 0–7879–6768–8

"Tim Stuart and Cheryl Bostrom offer a unique and practical perspective on how to have a godly, eternal impact on children. Their message is especially critical to those young people whose lives have been characterized by disappointment and rejection."
—Dr. Bill Bright, founder, Campus Crusade for Christ

"Every child is bound to bump into tough times and these experiences are sure to shape their character for good or ill. *Children At Promise* is an immensely practical and inspirational tool for helping kids rise above adversity—and succeed not only in spite of it, but because of it. This book is a winner!"
—Les Parrott, Ph.D., professor of clinical psychology, Seattle Pacific University; author, *Helping Your Struggling Teenager*

"Teachers of every stripe, public and private, will benefit from *Children At Promise*. Taken seriously, it would revolutionize American education. Every prospective and practicing parent and teacher will want to read this book. I needed this thirty-five years ago when I started teaching, and before I became a principal and a parent."
—Ron Polinder, executive director, Rehoboth Christian School

In today's complex world filled with violence, drugs, and confusing sexual messages, these and other threats to our young people have prompted educators, politicians, and government agencies to label our children as "at risk" of failure. Although intended to be a way of identifying those who need help, this label can cause us to taint our language and behaviors toward young people with hopelessness and defeat. But there is hope. *Children At Promise* maintains that all children can be viewed with positive expectancy and shows how we parents, grandparents, educators, and friends can help to fulfill our children's deep potential. In this inspirational and informative book, high school principal Tim Stuart, Ed.D. and former teacher-of-the-year Cheryl Bostrom, M.A., offer easy-to-understand, research-based evidence for the power of nurturing the promise in all children regardless of the risks they experience. Stuart and Bostrom's unique, revolutionary approach to child rearing emphasizes the true identity of all children and their caregivers, the importance of relationship, and the value of adversity. Solidly grounded in tested educational and psychological theory as well as with timeless biblical wisdom, *Children At Promise* provides parents and educators with the insights, motivation, and tools for raising successful children of P.R.O.M.I.S.E. character.